Thai Sou

Elevate Your Culinary Skills with Authentic Thai Recipes

HOPE CARLSON

Limited Liability Disclaimer

The information provided in the book "Thai Soup Secret: Elevate Your Culinary Skills with Authentic Thai Recipes" is intended for general informational purposes only. While every effort has been made to ensure the accuracy and completeness of the content, the author and publisher do not assume any responsibility for errors, inaccuracies, or omissions.

Readers are encouraged to use their discretion and seek professional advice if needed, especially in cases of dietary restrictions, allergies, or health concerns. The recipes and techniques shared in this book are based on the author's experience and research, and individual results may vary.

The author and publisher disclaim any liability for any loss, injury, or damage incurred as a direct or indirect consequence of the use or application of any information presented in this book. Readers are responsible for their own actions and should exercise caution when attempting new cooking techniques or experimenting with ingredients.

Furthermore, the author and publisher do not endorse any specific brands, products, or services mentioned in the book. Any reference to such entities is for illustrative purposes only and does not constitute an endorsement.

By using the information provided in this book, readers acknowledge and agree to the terms of this limited liability disclaimer. The author and publisher shall not be held liable for any direct, indirect, incidental, consequential, or punitive damages arising from the use of the information contained herein. Readers should use their best judgment and consult relevant professionals when in doubt.

This limited liability disclaimer is subject to change without notice. It is the responsibility of the reader to stay informed about any updates or modifications to these terms.

TABLE OF CONTENTS

Introduction

Brief overview of Thai cuisine and its cultural significance

Thai cuisine stands as a testament to the rich cultural tapestry that defines Thailand, blending flavours, aromas, and techniques with a history deeply rooted in tradition. This brief overview aims to unravel the layers of Thai culinary artistry and highlight its profound cultural significance.

At the heart of Thai cuisine lies a harmonious balance of four fundamental flavours: sweet, salty, sour, and spicy. This balance is not only a culinary principle but a reflection of the broader Thai cultural philosophy, emphasizing equilibrium and harmony in all aspects of life. Thai cuisine's intricate dance of flavours is meticulously crafted, transforming simple ingredients into a symphony for the taste buds.

One of the key elements that define Thai dishes is the creative use of herbs and spices. Garlic, ginger, lime, and chilli form the aromatic foundation, infusing every dish with a tantalizing fragrance. Beyond these basics, Thai chefs masterfully incorporate an array of aromatic herbs like basil, coriander, and mint, elevating each bite to a sensory experience. This aromatic diversity is not only a testament to the country's abundant natural resources but also a reflection of the Thai people's deep connection with their land.

Culinary rituals in Thailand extend far beyond the act of eating. The preparation of food is considered an art form, with each chef infusing their creations with a piece of their identity. The process of crafting a Thai meal often involves time-honoured techniques passed down through generations, ensuring that the essence of tradition is preserved in every dish. From the bustling street markets to the serene kitchens of Thai households, the art of cooking is a celebration of culture and community.

Regional diversity further enriches Thai cuisine, with each part of the country contributing its unique flavours and specialities. The North boasts hearty and earthy dishes, influenced by the mountainous terrain, while the South's coastal abundance is reflected in its vibrant seafood-centric offerings. Central Thailand, including Bangkok, serves as a culinary crossroads, blending regional flavours into a dynamic and diverse cuisine.

Beyond its exquisite taste, Thai cuisine plays a pivotal role in social gatherings and rituals. Sharing a meal is a symbolic act of unity, and Thai hospitality is expressed through the generosity of portions and the warmth with which guests are welcomed. Festivals and ceremonies often centre around special dishes, reinforcing the deep connection between food and cultural traditions.

Street food, a ubiquitous element of Thai culinary culture, deserves special mention. Night markets come alive with the sizzle of woks and the irresistible aroma of grilling meats. From the iconic Pad Thai to the fiery Som Tum (green papaya salad), street food is a direct portal to the heart of Thai culinary innovation, offering a diverse and accessible array of flavours to locals and visitors alike.

Contextualization of authentic Thai recipes as a key to elevating culinary skills

The exploration of authentic Thai recipes serves as a culinary odyssey, unlocking not only the secrets of exquisite flavours but also offering a unique opportunity to elevate one's culinary skills. Thai cuisine, renowned for its harmonious blend of sweet, salty, sour, and spicy elements, provides a gateway for aspiring chefs and home cooks to delve into the intricacies of flavour pairing, ingredient selection, and cooking techniques.

Authentic Thai recipes serve as a bridge between culinary enthusiasts and the rich cultural heritage of Thailand. Beyond the confines of a mere collection of instructions, these recipes are windows into the heart of Thai culinary philosophy. The importance of fresh, high-quality ingredients is paramount, echoing the Thai commitment to wholesome, flavorful meals. Contextualizing these recipes involves understanding not only the ingredients themselves but also the cultural significance they hold in the tapestry of Thai life.

The elevation of culinary skills begins with an appreciation for the foundational elements of Thai cuisine. Garlic, ginger, lime, and chilli form the backbone of many Thai dishes, infusing them with a depth of flavour that is both distinctive and nuanced. Aspiring chefs learn not only to wield these ingredients with precision but also to understand the alchemy that occurs when they come together in perfect harmony. The contextualization of these basics extends beyond the kitchen, connecting practitioners to the agricultural practices, regional variations, and historical context that shape Thai culinary traditions.

Moreover, authentic Thai recipes act as culinary storytellers, narrating tales of the diverse regions and communities that contribute to Thailand's gastronomic mosaic. From the aromatic curries of the central plains to the seafood-infused delights of the coastal regions, each recipe carries a sense of place and tradition. Understanding the regional nuances becomes a journey in itself, providing a broader context for the flavours that grace the Thai table.

Culinary elevation also involves the mastery of techniques unique to Thai cooking. The art of crafting a perfect curry paste, the skilful balance of flavours in a spicy Tom Yum soup, or the finesse required to prepare a Pad Thai that captures the essence of Thai street food – these are the challenges that beckon culinary enthusiasts to refine their skills. The journey is not just about replicating recipes; it is about embracing the philosophy that underpins each dish, a philosophy that values precision, balance, and a deep respect for the ingredients.

In the realm of Thai cuisine, authenticity is not a mere label but a commitment to preserving tradition. Contextualizing authentic Thai recipes involves recognizing the cultural rituals, seasonal influences, and culinary customs that shape the way these recipes are prepared and enjoyed. It's an invitation to step into the shoes of a Thai chef, understanding the thoughtfulness that goes into each step of the cooking process.

As culinary skills are honed through the exploration of authentic Thai recipes, individuals embark on a transformative journey. They not only become proficient in creating delicious meals but also develop a heightened awareness of the cultural significance of food. Thai cuisine, with its emphasis on balance and harmony, imparts not just technical expertise but a broader understanding of the role food plays in fostering connections, celebrating diversity, and creating shared experiences.

Preview of regional nuances and key ingredients
The magic of Thai cuisine unfolds in its regional diversity, with each part of the country contributing its unique flavours, techniques, and key ingredients. As we embark on a culinary journey through the regional nuances of Thailand, we discover a tapestry of tastes that reflects the geographical and cultural richness of this Southeast Asian nation.

Northern Thailand: The mountainous landscapes of Northern Thailand give rise to a distinctive culinary identity characterized by heartiness and earthiness. Key ingredients in Northern Thai cuisine include sticky rice, often used in place of regular rice, and an abundance of herbs like dill and mint. Dishes like "Khao Soi," a curry noodle soup, showcase the influence of neighbouring countries and the use of bold, aromatic spices. The cuisine of the North is a testament to resourcefulness, with ingredients like bamboo shoots, forest mushrooms, and game meat making regular appearances.

Central Thailand: The central plains, home to bustling Bangkok, serve as a culinary crossroads where regional flavours converge. Here, key ingredients include fragrant jasmine rice, freshwater fish, and an array of aromatic herbs. Central Thai cuisine is known for its balance of sweet, salty, and sour flavours. Dishes like the iconic "Pad Thai," a stir-fried noodle dish, and "Tom Yum Goong," a spicy shrimp soup, epitomize the harmonious blend of these tastes. The region's fertile plains contribute to a vibrant array of fruits and vegetables that grace the tables of both street vendors and fine-dining establishments.

Southern Thailand: The lush coastal landscapes of Southern Thailand bring forth a bounty of seafood that defines the region's culinary offerings. Coconut milk, palm sugar, and an abundance of fresh herbs characterize Southern Thai cuisine. Spices play a prominent role, with dishes like "Gaeng Som Pla," a sour fish curry, showcasing the bold and fiery flavours the region is known for. Influences from neighbouring Malaysia and Indonesia are evident, creating a unique fusion that sets Southern Thai cuisine apart. The use of turmeric, lemongrass, and galangal adds layers of complexity to dishes, creating a symphony of flavours.

Northeastern Thailand (Isan): Isan cuisine, hailing from the northeastern region, is renowned for its bold and spicy profiles. Sticky rice is a staple, often accompanied by grilled meats, fiery chilli dips, and an abundance of fresh herbs. Key ingredients include the aromatic herb "kaffir lime leaves" and the fiery "bird's eye chilli," which imparts a distinctive heat to many Isan dishes. "Som Tum," a green papaya salad, exemplifies the region's love for vibrant, spicy flavours. Isan cuisine reflects the resourcefulness of the land, with dishes that celebrate local ingredients and traditional preparation methods.

Understanding these regional nuances is essential for anyone seeking to authentically replicate Thai recipes. It goes beyond the mere combination of ingredients, providing insight into the historical, cultural, and geographical factors that have shaped each culinary tradition. The regional diversity of Thai cuisine is a testament to the country's ability to transform humble ingredients into culinary masterpieces, creating a dynamic and ever-evolving food culture.

As we delve into the rich tapestry of regional nuances and key ingredients, we discover that Thai cuisine is not a monolithic entity but a mosaic of flavours, a reflection of the diverse landscapes and communities that define this captivating nation. Each bite is an invitation to explore the nuances of Thai culture, offering a sensory journey that transcends the boundaries of geography and brings the essence of Thailand to our plates.

Chapter 1: "Aromatic Foundations of Thai Cuisine"

Description of fundamental elements of Thai cuisine: garlic, ginger, lime, chilli

Thai cuisine, a culinary symphony that has captivated taste buds around the world, derives its vibrant and complex flavours from a handful of fundamental elements. At the core of this culinary artistry lie four essential ingredients: garlic, ginger, lime, and chilli. Each of these elements plays a pivotal role in shaping the distinctiveness of Thai dishes, contributing to the harmonious balance of sweet, salty, sour, and spicy flavours that define this rich and diverse culinary tradition.

Garlic: Garlic, a ubiquitous component in Thai cuisine, serves as a foundation for many savoury dishes. Its aromatic and pungent notes infuse depth and richness into curries, stir-fries, and soups. Whether minced, sliced, or pounded into a paste, garlic adds a robust and earthy flavour that forms the backbone of countless Thai recipes. Beyond its culinary significance, garlic holds cultural importance, believed by many to possess medicinal properties. Thai chefs skillfully wield garlic to create layers of complexity, ensuring that its presence is felt without overpowering the overall harmony of the dish.

Ginger: Another cornerstone of Thai cuisine is ginger, valued for its warm and slightly spicy undertones. Fresh ginger, often sliced or finely chopped, imparts a zesty kick to dishes, while galangal, a close relative with a more citrusy and piney flavour, adds a unique dimension to Thai curries. Both forms of ginger are integral to the balance of flavours, providing a counterpoint to the richness of coconut milk and the heat of the chilli. In Thai cuisine, ginger is not just a spice; it's a dynamic element that contributes to the complexity and depth of taste, making each bite a sensory experience.

Lime: The zesty acidity of lime is a hallmark of Thai cuisine, introducing a burst of freshness that cuts through richer flavours. Lime juice is a versatile ingredient, used to balance the richness of coconut-based curries, enhance the sweetness of desserts, and add a tangy kick to salads. The aromatic zest of lime also finds its way into many recipes, amplifying the citrusy notes and contributing to the olfactory allure of Thai dishes. In addition to its culinary role, lime holds cultural significance, symbolizing purity and cleansing in Thai traditions.

Chilli: No discussion of Thai cuisine would be complete without highlighting the fiery kick of chilli, a key player in the realm of spice. Thai cuisine masterfully wields chilli to create a spectrum of heat, from mild to intense. The small but potent Thai bird's eye chilli is a favourite, delivering a concentrated punch of spiciness. The use of chilli is not merely about adding heat; it's about achieving the delicate balance of flavours that Thai cuisine is celebrated for. The heat from chilli is carefully calibrated to complement the other elements, creating a symphony where each note is in perfect harmony.

Together, these fundamental elements form the backbone of Thai culinary alchemy. They are the building blocks upon which the intricate layers of flavour are constructed, showcasing the artful skill of Thai chefs in balancing contrasting tastes. Beyond their individual contributions, these ingredients represent a holistic approach to cooking, where each component is carefully selected to enhance the overall dining experience.

As one delves into the world of Thai cuisine, the appreciation for these fundamental elements deepens. Garlic, ginger, lime, and chilli are not just ingredients; they are storytellers, narrating tales of tradition, culture, and the vibrant landscapes of Thailand. They embody the essence of Thai culinary philosophy, where the art of balance transforms a simple meal into a sensory journey, inviting all who partake to savour the rich and nuanced flavours of this culinary treasure.

Exploration of aromatic herbs like basil, coriander, and mint

The aromatic herbs of Thai cuisine constitute a fragrant and enchanting symphony that elevates the culinary experience to extraordinary heights. Among these, basil, coriander, and mint stand out as pillars of flavour, each lending its unique essence to Thai dishes. The exploration of these aromatic herbs not only adds depth and complexity to the cuisine but also unveils the cultural significance and culinary prowess that characterize Thai gastronomy.

Basil: Thai basil, with its distinctive anise-like flavour and bold, spicy notes, is a cornerstone of Thai herbology. Varieties such as holy basil (bai grow) and sweet basil (bai horapa) are employed in different dishes, imparting their aromatic richness. Holy basil, with its peppery undertones, takes a lead role in iconic dishes like "Pad Krapow," a stir-fry that exemplifies the harmonious interplay of basil, garlic, and chilli. The fragrance of Thai basil permeates the air in bustling street markets and home kitchens alike, infusing every bite with an unmistakable and tantalizing aroma.

Coriander: Coriander, in its various forms – leaves, stems, and seeds – is a multifaceted herb that contributes both flavour and visual appeal to Thai cuisine. Fresh coriander leaves, also known as cilantro, are a ubiquitous garnish, adding a burst of citrusy freshness to soups, curries, and salads. Coriander stems, often finely chopped, find their way into aromatic pastes and marinades, enhancing the overall complexity of many Thai dishes. The seeds, ground into a powder, bring a warm and citrusy nuance to spice blends. The use of coriander in Thai cooking reflects the country's deep-rooted connection with herbal diversity and the art of layering flavours.

Mint: Mint, with its cool and refreshing profile, is a surprising but delightful addition to Thai cuisine. Peppermint and spearmint varieties are used to infuse dishes with a bright, aromatic lift. Mint leaves find their place in salads, desserts, and savoury dishes, imparting a burst of coolness that balances the heat of chillies. "Yam," Thai salads that showcase the vibrant combination of herbs, often feature mint as a key player, adding a dynamic element to the ensemble. The inclusion of mint reflects the Thai culinary philosophy of creating dishes that engage all the senses, marrying unexpected flavours for a truly sensory experience.

The exploration of these aromatic herbs extends beyond their individual contributions; it delves into the cultural and holistic approach to wellness that defines Thai culinary traditions. Thai cuisine values not only the flavour these herbs impart but also their aromatic and medicinal qualities. The use of herbs in Thai cooking is not merely a culinary choice; it's a reflection of the country's rich botanical heritage and the belief in the holistic benefits of incorporating herbs into daily meals.

In Thai culture, herbs are revered for their therapeutic properties, believed to promote well-being and balance. The aromatic herbs used in Thai cuisine aren't just seasonings; they are herbal allies that contribute to the overall health and vitality of those who partake in the dishes. This cultural connection to the healing properties of herbs adds another layer of depth to the exploration, showcasing the interconnectedness of culinary traditions and holistic well-being in Thai culinary philosophy.

As one embarks on the exploration of aromatic herbs like basil, coriander, and mint in Thai cuisine, it becomes evident that these elements are more than culinary embellishments. They are conduits to a rich cultural tapestry, carrying stories of tradition, healing, and the profound connection between nature and nourishment. The aromatic herbs of Thai cuisine, with their symphony of scents and flavours, beckon culinary enthusiasts to embark on a sensory journey that transcends the boundaries of taste, providing a glimpse into the essence of Thai culinary mastery.

Recipe: "Tom Yum Goong" - Spicy shrimp soup

In the realm of Thai culinary masterpieces, "Tom Yum Goong" stands out as an iconic and exhilarating expression of the country's renowned flavours. This spicy shrimp soup is a symphony of bold and harmonious tastes, showcasing the intricate balance of sweet, sour, salty, and spicy elements that define Thai cuisine. As we embark on the exploration of this celebrated recipe, we unravel the layers of complexity that make Tom Yum Goong a culinary treasure.

Ingredients:

1. **Shrimp:** The star of the show, fresh shrimp brings a delicate sweetness to the soup. The choice of succulent, perfectly cooked shrimp is crucial to the dish's success.

2. **Tom Yum Paste:** A fragrant blend of lemongrass, galangal, kaffir lime leaves, shallots, chilli, and other aromatic herbs, Tom Yum paste forms the flavorful base of the soup. This paste encapsulates the essence of Thai herbs and spices.

3. **Broth:** The foundation of Tom Yum Goong is a broth that marries the richness of chicken

or fish stock with the citrusy zing of lime juice. The broth is a canvas for the infusion of flavours from herbs and spices.

4. **Lime:** Fresh lime juice adds a vibrant acidity that cuts through the richness of the broth, providing a refreshing contrast and enhancing the overall complexity of the soup.

5. **Fish Sauce:** A key umami component, fish sauce adds depth and saltiness to the soup. It is a fundamental seasoning in Thai cuisine and plays a pivotal role in achieving the perfect balance of flavours.

6. **Chili:** The heat in Tom Yum Goong comes from Thai bird's eye chilli, which imparts a fiery kick to the soup. The level of spiciness can be adjusted according to personal preference.

7. **Herbs:** Kaffir lime leaves and lemongrass add citrusy and floral notes, while Thai basil contributes its distinctive anise-like flavour. The inclusion of these herbs elevates the soup's aroma and provides a refreshing herbal backdrop.

Cooking Process:

1. **Prepare the Broth:** Begin by bringing chicken or fish stock to a simmer. Infuse the broth with the Tom Yum paste, allowing the aromatic herbs and spices to permeate the liquid.

2. **Add Shrimp:** Once the broth is infused, introduce the fresh shrimp. The shrimp cook quickly and absorb the flavours of the broth, becoming tender and flavorful.

3. **Seasoning:** Balance is key in Tom Yum Goong. Add fish sauce for saltiness, lime juice for acidity, and Thai bird's eye chilli for heat. Adjust these components to achieve the desired taste profile.

4. **Herbs and Aromatics:** Introduce kaffir lime leaves, lemongrass, and Thai basil to the simmering soup. These herbs infuse the dish with their aromatic essence, creating a multi-dimensional flavour experience.

5. **Serve Hot:** Tom Yum Goong is traditionally served piping hot, allowing the steam to carry an enticing aroma to the eager diner. Garnish with fresh cilantro and sliced chilli for a visually appealing presentation.

Culinary Experience: The beauty of Tom Yum Goong lies not only in its taste but also in the sensory journey it offers. As you take the first spoonful, the fragrant steam envelops your senses, foretelling the symphony of flavours that await. The initial heat from the chilli is tempered by the sweetness of the shrimp, while the tangy lime juice dances on the palate. Each ingredient plays its part in creating a dynamic and exhilarating experience, showcasing the Thai philosophy of balance and harmony.

Beyond its delectable taste, Tom Yum Goong reflects the spirit of Thai cuisine – a celebration of fresh, quality ingredients and a commitment to the art of flavour alchemy. The dish embodies the cultural reverence for herbs and spices, transforming a humble soup into a culinary masterpiece that resonates with food enthusiasts worldwide.

Chapter 2: "The Art of Thai Curry Preparation"

Exploration of different Thai curry varieties: red, green, yellow

The exploration of Thai curry varieties is a tantalizing journey through a spectrum of flavours, colours, and aromatic spices that define the rich tapestry of Thai cuisine. Red, green, and yellow curries, each with its unique characteristics, offer a sensorial experience that reflects the culinary artistry and regional influences of Thailand. As we delve into the distinct profiles of these Thai curry varieties, we uncover the secrets that make each one a masterpiece in its own right.

Red Curry: Red curry is a fiery and robust variety that derives its vibrant colour and intense heat from red chilli peppers. The base of the curry paste includes a medley of ingredients such as lemongrass, galangal, garlic, shallots, coriander roots, and shrimp paste. The result is a complex and aromatic paste that infuses the curry with layers of flavour. Red curry commonly features meat – such as chicken, beef, or pork – or seafood, along with bamboo shoots, Thai eggplant, and sweet basil. The coconut milk in red curry provides a creamy richness that tempers the spiciness, creating a harmonious balance between heat and velvety texture.

Green Curry: Green curry, known for its verdant hue and vibrant, herbaceous flavour, gets its colour from fresh green chilli peppers. The curry paste includes not only green chillies but also ingredients like lemongrass, coriander, kaffir lime leaves, and Thai basil, contributing to its distinctive aroma. Green curry often features chicken or fish, along with vegetables like zucchini, eggplant, and peas. The use of Thai basil gives the curry a refreshing and slightly peppery undertone. Green curry is renowned for its bold and invigorating taste, making it a favourite among those who appreciate a lively and aromatic dining experience.

Yellow Curry: Yellow curry, with its warm and comforting golden hue, is a milder variety that offers a delightful balance of flavours. Turmeric is the key ingredient responsible for the curry's colour, while the curry paste incorporates a blend of spices such as cumin, coriander, and cinnamon. The resulting flavour profile is both fragrant and mildly spicy. Yellow curry often features meat, such as chicken or beef, along with potatoes and carrots. The creaminess of coconut milk complements the spices, creating a smooth and velvety texture. Yellow curry stands out for its gentle heat and aromatic complexity, making it an excellent choice for those who prefer a milder yet flavorful curry experience.

The diversity of Thai curry varieties goes beyond their ingredients; it reflects the regional influences that shape the culinary landscape of Thailand. Each curry tells a story of the ingredients abundant in its region, the culinary traditions of the local communities, and the creative flair of Thai chefs. Understanding the nuances of these curry varieties allows for a deeper appreciation of the cultural and geographical diversity that defines Thai cuisine.

Thai curries are not just dishes; they are a culinary philosophy that celebrates the art of balance. The interplay between spices, herbs, and proteins in each curry variety exemplifies the Thai commitment to achieving a harmonious blend of flavours. The contrast of spicy, sweet, and savoury notes in Thai curries showcases the country's culinary mastery, where every ingredient plays a vital role in creating a symphony of tastes that captivates the palate.

As one explores the different Thai curry varieties – red, green, and yellow – it becomes evident that these dishes are more than a collection of ingredients; they are an invitation to embark on a flavorful journey. Whether savouring the heat of red curry, revelling in the herbaceous richness of green curry, or delighting in the comforting warmth of yellow curry, each variety offers a unique and unforgettable experience, transporting diners to the vibrant heart of Thai gastronomy.

Guide to homemade curry paste preparation
Embarking on the journey of homemade curry paste preparation is a culinary adventure that unveils the essence of Thai cuisine in its purest form. Crafting your own curry paste allows you to immerse yourself in the aromatic symphony of fresh herbs, spices, and vibrant flavours that define Thai culinary artistry. As we delve into the guide for homemade curry paste, we discover the secrets behind this essential element that forms the backbone of countless Thai dishes.

Ingredients: The beauty of homemade curry paste lies in the quality and freshness of its ingredients. While store-bought options are convenient, crafting your own paste offers a level of control over the flavour profile that is unparalleled. Common ingredients include:

1. **Chilies:** The heat level can be adjusted based on personal preference. Thai bird's eye chillies provide an authentic spiciness.

2. **Lemongrass:** With its citrusy fragrance, lemongrass adds a bright and zesty note to the paste.

3. **Galangal:** A rhizome similar to ginger but with a more peppery and citrusy flavour, galangal is a key aromatic element.

4. **Shallots and Garlic:** These aromatic bulbs form the savoury foundation of the paste, contributing depth and complexity.

5. **Coriander Roots:** Often overlooked, coriander roots pack an intense flavour and are a traditional addition to Thai curry pastes.

6. **Kaffir Lime Leaves:** With their unique citrusy aroma, kaffir lime leaves lend a distinctive fragrance to the paste.

7. **Cumin and Coriander Seeds:** These toasted seeds add warm, earthy notes and enhance the overall complexity of the paste.

8. **Shrimp Paste:** A small amount of shrimp paste provides umami and depth, though it can be omitted for a vegetarian version.

Preparation:

1. **Chilies and Aromatics:** Begin by deseeding the chillies if you prefer a milder paste. Then, finely chop the chillies, lemongrass, galangal, shallots, and garlic. For an authentic touch, pound them in a mortar and pestle to release their essential oils and create a paste-like consistency.

2. **Spices:** Toast the coriander and cumin seeds in a dry pan until fragrant, then grind them into a powder. This step intensifies their flavours and contributes a depth of warmth to the curry paste.

3. **Combining Ingredients:** In a blender or mortar and pestle, combine all the chopped aromatics, ground spices, coriander roots, kaffir lime leaves, and shrimp paste. Blend or pound until a smooth paste forms. The key is achieving a homogeneous mixture that captures the essence of each ingredient.

4. **Adjusting Consistency:** Depending on the recipe you're preparing, you may need to adjust the consistency of the paste. For some dishes, a thick, concentrated paste is ideal, while others benefit from a looser, more liquid consistency. This adaptability is one of the advantages of homemade curry paste.

5. **Storing:** Homemade curry paste can be stored in an airtight container in the refrigerator for up to a week. For longer storage, freeze portions in an ice cube tray for convenient use in future recipes.

Culinary Experience: The act of preparing your own curry paste is not just a culinary task; it's an immersive experience that connects you with the heart of Thai cooking. The vibrant colours, aromatic fragrances, and the tactile process of grinding and blending create a sensory journey that goes beyond the final dish.

The flavours captured in homemade curry paste are unparalleled, offering a depth and authenticity that commercial alternatives may lack. Each spoonful carries the essence of fresh herbs, pungent aromatics, and the craftsmanship of your hands. The result is not just a paste; it's a testament to the art of Thai culinary tradition, where the act of creating a dish is as significant as its consumption.

Beyond the immediate gratification of a delicious curry, homemade paste provides the foundation for endless culinary explorations. Its versatility extends beyond curries to marinades, stir-fries, and even dips, allowing you to infuse a myriad of dishes with an unmistakable Thai flavour profile.

Recipe: "Gaeng Keow Wan Gai" - Green chicken curry

Embarking on the culinary adventure of preparing "Gaeng Keow Wan Gai," or Green Chicken Curry, is a delightful journey into the heart of Thai cuisine. This iconic dish is a symphony of flavours, blending the vibrant hues of fresh herbs with the creamy richness of coconut milk. As we explore the recipe for Green Chicken Curry, we unravel the secrets behind this culinary masterpiece that has captivated palates around the world.

Ingredients:

1. Chicken: Use boneless, skinless chicken thighs or breasts, cut into bite-sized pieces. The

choice of chicken ensures a tender and succulent texture.

2. Green Curry Paste: Craft your own homemade green curry paste for an authentic touch, using ingredients like green chillies, lemongrass, galangal, kaffir lime leaves, and coriander roots. Alternatively, you can use a high-quality store-bought version.

3. Coconut Milk: The luscious creaminess of coconut milk is a hallmark of Thai curries. Opt for a good-quality, full-fat coconut milk to impart richness to the curry.

4. Vegetables: Green Chicken Curry typically includes Thai eggplant, bamboo shoots, and sweet basil. These vegetables add texture, flavour, and a touch of sweetness to the dish.

5. Fish Sauce: A key element in Thai cuisine, fish sauce provides the savoury depth that is fundamental to the balance of flavours in the curry.

6. Palm Sugar: To add a subtle sweetness to the curry, palm sugar is used. Adjust the amount based on personal preference.

7. Kaffir Lime Leaves: These aromatic leaves, finely shredded, infuse the curry with a citrusy fragrance and contribute to its distinctive flavour.

8. Thai Basil: Fresh Thai basil leaves add a peppery and anise-like note, enhancing the overall herbal complexity of the dish.

Cooking Process:

1. Prepare the Green Curry Paste: If making your own paste, follow the steps outlined in the homemade curry paste preparation guide. Otherwise, ensure that your store-bought paste is ready for use.

2. Sauté the Curry Paste: In a pot or wok, heat a small amount of coconut milk over medium heat. Add the green curry paste and sauté until it becomes fragrant, releasing its aromatic oils.

3. Add Chicken: Introduce the bite-sized chicken pieces to the curry paste, coating them evenly. Allow the chicken to brown slightly on all sides, absorbing the flavours of the paste.

4. Pour Coconut Milk: Once the chicken is seared, pour in the remaining coconut milk, creating a velvety base for the curry. Bring the mixture to a gentle simmer.

5. Incorporate Vegetables: Add Thai eggplant, bamboo shoots, and shredded kaffir lime leaves to the simmering curry. These vegetables contribute texture and absorb the flavours of the curry.

6. Season with Fish Sauce and Palm Sugar: Enhance the savoury depth of the curry with

fish sauce, adjusting the quantity to achieve the desired saltiness. Add palm sugar to balance the flavours, creating a harmonious blend of sweet and savoury.

7. Simmer to Perfection: Allow the curry to simmer gently, letting the chicken become tender and the vegetables absorb the aromatic essence of the coconut-infused broth.

8. Finish with Thai Basil: Just before serving, stir in fresh Thai basil leaves, infusing the curry with their aromatic peppery notes. This last addition adds a burst of freshness to the dish.

9. Serve Hot: Gaeng Keow Wan Gai is traditionally served hot, accompanied by steamed jasmine rice. The aromatic steam rising from the vibrant green curry is a prelude to the delightful flavours that await.

Culinary Experience: The culinary experience of indulging in Green Chicken Curry is a celebration of Thailand's rich gastronomic heritage. Each spoonful offers a burst of herbal freshness, a hint of sweetness, and a velvety richness that exemplifies the artful balance of Thai flavours.

Beyond its delectable taste, Green Chicken Curry embodies the spirit of Thai hospitality and the philosophy of creating dishes that engage all the senses. The vibrant green colour, aromatic fragrance, and interplay of textures create a multisensory experience that goes beyond the boundaries of a mere meal.

The versatility of Green Chicken Curry extends to various occasions – from cosy family dinners to festive gatherings. It's a dish that can be tailored to individual preferences, allowing for adjustments in spice levels, sweetness, and the selection of vegetables.

Chapter 3: "Night Market Street Food"

Dive into vibrant Thai night markets and their culinary offerings

Diving into the vibrant tapestry of Thai night markets is an exhilarating journey that immerses visitors in a kaleidoscope of colours, aromas, and flavours. These bustling nocturnal hubs, scattered across Thailand, serve as more than just places to procure goods; they are lively showcases of the country's culinary diversity, offering a tantalizing array of street food and local delicacies. As we explore Thai night markets and their culinary offerings, we unveil the cultural richness and gastronomic treasures that define this unique aspect of Thailand's culinary landscape.

The Atmosphere: Thai night markets come alive as the sun sets, transforming bustling streets into vibrant hubs of activity. The air is infused with the sizzle of grills, the enticing fragrance of spices, and the lively chatter of vendors and patrons. Colourful lights illuminate the scene, creating an electrifying ambience that beckons locals and tourists alike. The atmosphere is a harmonious blend of commerce, community, and culinary artistry, making it a quintessential Thai experience.

Street Food Galore: At the heart of Thai night markets lies an astonishing array of street food stalls, each presenting a cornucopia of flavours that span the entire spectrum of Thai cuisine. From savory to sweet, and mild to fiery, the options are as diverse as the country's culinary heritage. Grilled meats on skewers, aromatic noodle dishes, flavorful curries, and tantalizing desserts beckon those seeking an authentic taste of Thailand.

Signature Dishes: Night markets are treasure troves of signature Thai dishes that have gained international acclaim. Pad Thai, the iconic stir-fried noodle dish, is expertly prepared on sizzling woks, infusing the air with the aroma of tamarind, fish sauce, and peanuts. Som Tum, a refreshing green papaya salad, is crafted with a perfect balance of sweet, sour, and spicy elements. The rich and creamy Coconut Ice

Cream, served in coconut shells and adorned with an assortment of toppings, offers a cool respite from the tropical heat.

Regional Specialties: One of the unique aspects of Thai night markets is the opportunity to savour regional specialities from different parts of the country. Whether it's the aromatic Northern Thai curries, the spicy Isan dishes from the Northeast, or the seafood delights of the coastal regions, night markets act as culinary crossroads where diverse flavours converge. Exploring these regional nuances allows visitors to embark on a gastronomic journey that spans the entire geography of Thailand.

Vendor Expertise: The vendors themselves are often local experts, passing down recipes through generations and perfecting their craft over years of hands-on experience. These culinary artisans take pride in their creations, showcasing not only their skills but also the regional identity embedded in each dish. Engaging with vendors becomes a cultural exchange, where a simple meal becomes a window into the heart of Thai traditions.

Culinary Innovation: Beyond traditional favourites, Thai night markets are hubs of culinary innovation. Creative twists on classic dishes, fusion flavours, and inventive presentations characterize the dynamic nature of street food. Vendors push culinary boundaries, introducing new and exciting combinations that reflect Thailand's contemporary culinary landscape.

Community and Socializing: Thai night markets are not just about food; they are communal spaces that foster socializing and community engagement. Locals and visitors alike gather around communal tables, sharing stories and laughter as they indulge in the diverse array of dishes. The communal experience enhances the enjoyment of the culinary adventure, creating lasting memories for those who partake.

Tips for Night Market Exploration:

1. **Come Hungry:** The abundance of tempting options demands an appetite. Arrive with an empty stomach and a sense of culinary curiosity.

2. **Embrace Adventure:** Be adventurous in your choices. Try dishes you may not have encountered before, and don't shy away from experimenting with flavours.

3. **Engage with Vendors:** Strike up conversations with the vendors. Learn about the history and inspiration behind their dishes. Many vendors are eager to share their culinary expertise and local insights.

4. **Sample Locally:** Look for stalls where locals are queuing up. This is often a sign of authenticity and quality.

5. **Go Beyond Food:** While food is a highlight, Thai night markets also offer a variety of goods, from handmade crafts to clothing and accessories. Explore the market beyond the culinary section to discover unique finds.

Exploration of iconic street food dishes like Pad Thai and Som Tu

Embarking on an exploration of iconic Thai street food dishes like Pad Thai and Som Tum is a gastronomic journey that unveils the heart and soul of Thailand's culinary landscape. These beloved street eats are more than just meals; they are cultural ambassadors, representing the vibrant flavours, aromatic spices, and culinary artistry that define Thai cuisine. As we delve into the essence of Pad Thai and Som Tum, we discover the stories behind these street food classics and the sensory delights they offer to locals and visitors alike.

Pad Thai: The Quintessential Stir-Fried Noodles

Pad Thai, arguably Thailand's most famous street food export, is a harmonious blend of textures and flavours expertly woven together in a single work. This iconic dish features stir-fried rice noodles, creating a base that serves as a canvas for the symphony of ingredients that follow.

Ingredients:

1. **Rice Noodles:** Flat rice noodles, soaked until pliable and stir-fried to perfection, provide the foundation for Pad Thai.

2. **Protein:** Shrimp, chicken, or tofu are commonly used, contributing a protein-rich element to the dish.

3. **Tamarind Paste:** The distinctive sweet and sour notes in Pad Thai come from tamarind

paste, a key ingredient that defines its unique flavour profile.

4. **Fish Sauce:** Essential in Thai cuisine, the fish sauce adds depth and umami, enhancing the savoury character of Pad Thai.

5. **Bean Sprouts and Chives:** These crunchy and fresh elements contribute texture and a burst of freshness.

6. **Peanuts:** Crushed roasted peanuts provide a delightful crunch, adding a layer of complexity to the dish.

7. **Lime Wedges:** Served on the side, lime wedges offer a citrusy kick that brightens the overall flavour.

Culinary Experience: The culinary experience of Pad Thai goes beyond its delicious taste; it's a sensory journey that engages multiple senses. The sizzling of the work, the aromatic fragrance of tamarind and fish sauce, and the visual appeal of vibrant ingredients coming together create an immersive encounter. The final presentation, garnished with peanuts and lime, is not just a plate of noodles; it's a work of culinary art that encapsulates the essence of Thai street food.

Som Tum: The Refreshing Green Papaya Salad Som Tum, or green papaya salad, is a refreshing and zesty street food gem that embodies the lively and bold flavours of Thai cuisine. This salad is a masterful composition of fresh ingredients that deliver a symphony of sweet, sour, spicy, and savoury notes.

Ingredients:

1. **Green Papaya:** Shredded green papaya forms the crisp and refreshing base of the salad, providing a textural contrast to other ingredients.

2. **Chilies:** Thai bird's eye chillies contribute fiery heat, while the quantity can be adjusted to suit individual spice preferences.

3. **Garlic:** Freshly minced garlic adds a pungent kick that enhances the overall savoury profile of Som Tum.

4. **Fish Sauce:** A fundamental element in Thai cooking, fish sauce imparts depth and saltiness, creating a savoury foundation.

5. **Lime Juice:** Freshly squeezed lime juice adds a vibrant acidity that balances the richness of other flavours.

6. **Palm Sugar:** To counterbalance the heat and acidity, palm sugar is used to provide a subtle sweetness.

7. **Tomatoes and Peanuts:** Juicy cherry tomatoes and crushed peanuts contribute to the salad's complexity, offering bursts of sweetness and crunch.

Culinary Experience: Som Tum is not just a salad; it's a celebration of contrasts. The crispness of shredded papaya, the heat from chillies, the crunch of peanuts, and the citrusy brightness of lime create a dance of flavours that invigorates the palate. The tactile experience of pounding the ingredients in a mortar and pestle, a traditional method of preparation, adds an extra layer of authenticity to the culinary adventure.

Regional Variations and Beyond Both Pad Thai and Som Tum showcase the adaptability and diversity of Thai cuisine, with regional variations adding unique twists to these classics. In different parts of Thailand, you might encounter variations that highlight local ingredients, spice levels, or preparation methods, providing a nuanced exploration of the country's culinary tapestry.

Beyond Thailand's borders, Pad Thai and Som Tum have become global ambassadors of Thai street food. From bustling markets in Bangkok to food stalls in international cities, these dishes have transcended cultural boundaries, becoming beloved favourites that resonate with diverse palates.

Street Food as Cultural Heritage: Pad Thai and Som Tum, among other iconic street food dishes, are not just about nourishment; they embody the spirit of Thai culture and hospitality. They represent the tradition of communal dining, where locals and visitors gather around street stalls, forging connections over shared meals. The simplicity of street food belies the rich cultural heritage and culinary mastery embedded in each dish.

Culinary Exploration Tips:

1. **Try Local Variations:** When exploring Pad Thai and Som Tum, be open to trying local

variations. Different regions might incorporate unique ingredients or preparation techniques.

2. **Engage with Street Vendors:** Strike up conversations with street vendors. Their passion for their craft and local insights can enhance your culinary experience.

3. **Adjust Spice Levels:** Thai cuisine is known for its bold flavours, including spiciness. Feel free to communicate your spice preferences with vendors to tailor the dishes to your liking.

4. **Explore Street Food Markets:** Venture beyond renowned restaurants and explore street food markets. These vibrant hubs offer a more immersive experience, allowing you to witness the preparation of dishes and interact with locals.

Recipe: "Pad Krapow Moo" - Stir-fried rice with pork and basil

Delving into the culinary artistry of Thai cuisine, the recipe for "Pad Krapow Moo" – Stir-fried rice with pork and basil – offers a tantalizing journey into the heart of Thai street food. This iconic dish is a harmonious symphony of flavours, blending succulent pork, aromatic basil, and signature Thai seasonings that create a dish both vibrant and comforting. As we embark on the steps to create Pad Krapow Moo, we unveil the culinary secrets that make this street food classic a favourite among locals and global food enthusiasts alike.

Ingredients:

1. **Ground Pork:** Use high-quality ground pork to ensure a tender and flavorful protein base for the dish.

2. **Basil Leaves:** Thai holy basil is the star of Pad Krapow Moo, providing an aromatic and peppery flavour. If unavailable, regular basil can be a suitable substitute.

3. **Chilies:** Thai bird's eye chillies bring heat to the dish. Adjust the quantity based on personal spice preferences.

4. **Garlic:** Freshly minced garlic adds a savoury depth that complements the other flavours in the stir-fry.

5. **Fish Sauce:** A cornerstone of Thai cuisine, fish sauce imparts umami and saltiness, elevating the overall savoury profile of the dish.

6. **Soy Sauce:** Soy sauce contributes depth of flavour and a rich, salty element to the stir-fry.

7. **Oyster Sauce:** Providing a sweet and savoury component, the oyster sauce adds complexity to the dish.

8. **Sugar:** A touch of sugar balances the flavours, offering a hint of sweetness that harmonizes with the savoury and spicy notes.

9. **Vegetable Oil:** Use a neutral vegetable oil for stir-frying, allowing the ingredients to cook evenly.

10. **Rice:** Cooked jasmine rice serves as the base for Pad Krapow Moo, absorbing the flavorful juices of the stir-fry.

Cooking Process:

1. **Prepare Ingredients:** Mince the garlic, finely chop the Thai bird's eye chillies, and pluck the basil leaves from the stems. Have all ingredients ready and within reach for efficient stir-frying.

2. **Heat the Wok or Pan:** Place a wok or a large pan over high heat. Add a small amount of vegetable oil and let it heat until shimmering.

3. **Sauté Garlic and Chilies:** Add the minced garlic and chopped Thai chillies to the hot oil. Sauté briefly until the garlic becomes aromatic, taking care not to burn it.

4. **Add Ground Pork:** Introduce the ground pork to the wok, breaking it apart with a spatula. Stir-fry until the pork is cooked through and starts to brown, absorbing the fragrant flavours of garlic and chillies.

5. **Season with Fish Sauce, Soy Sauce, Oyster Sauce, and Sugar:** Pour in fish sauce, soy

sauce, and oyster sauce over the pork. Sprinkle sugar evenly across the mixture. Stir to combine, allowing the sauces to coat the pork and infuse it with savoury and sweet notes.

6. **Incorporate Basil Leaves:** Once the pork is cooked and coated in the flavorful sauces, add the fresh basil leaves to the wok. Toss the leaves into the stir-fry, allowing them to wilt slightly and release their aromatic essence.

7. **Taste and Adjust:** Taste the stir-fry and adjust the seasoning if needed. Additional fish sauce, soy sauce, or sugar can be added to achieve the desired balance of flavours.

8. **Serve Over Rice:** Spoon the Pad Krapow Moo over steamed jasmine rice on serving plates. The rice acts as a canvas, soaking up the savoury juices and providing a delightful textural contrast to the stir-fry.

Culinary Experience:

Pad Krapow Moo offers a culinary experience that engages the senses from the sizzling wok to the final forkful. The aroma of garlic, chillies, and basil wafts through the air, creating an anticipation of the flavours to come. The visual appeal is vibrant, with the basil leaves adding a pop of green to the golden-brown stir-fried pork. Each bite is a delightful dance of savoury, spicy, and aromatic notes, showcasing the quintessential balance of Thai cuisine.

Variations and Tips:

45

1. **Thai Holy Basil:** While Thai holy basil is the traditional choice for Pad Krapow Moo, regular basil can be used if the former is unavailable. The dish maintains its aromatic quality with the peppery notes of basil.

2. **Adjusting Spice Levels:** The quantity of Thai bird's eye chillies can be adjusted to suit personal spice preferences. For a milder version, reduce the number of chillies or remove the seeds.

3. **Protein Options:** While the recipe features ground pork, Pad Krapow can be prepared with other proteins such as chicken, beef, or tofu. Adjust the cooking time accordingly based on the chosen protein.

4. **Vegetable Additions:** Enhance the dish with the addition of vegetables like bell peppers, onions, or green beans. These additions contribute colour, texture, and nutritional value to the stir-fry.

5. **Garnish:** For a finishing touch, garnish the Pad Krapow Moo with additional basil leaves and a sprinkle of chopped chillies. This not only adds visual appeal but intensifies the aromatic experience.

Chapter 4: "The Balanced Dance of Thai Flavors"

Discussion on the importance of balancing sweet, salty, sour, and spicy flavours

The essence of Thai cuisine lies in its ability to harmonize a symphony of flavours, creating a culinary experience that tantalizes the taste buds and lingers in the memory. Central to this mastery is the importance of balancing sweet, salty, sour, and spicy elements in every dish. In Thai culinary philosophy, achieving this balance is not just a technique; it is an art form that reflects the country's rich cultural heritage, geographical diversity, and a deep understanding of flavour dynamics.

Sweetness: The inclusion of sweetness in Thai cuisine is not merely about satisfying a sweet tooth; it serves as a counterpoint to the savoury and spicy components, creating a multidimensional palate. Palm sugar, a common sweetener in Thai cooking, imparts a subtle sweetness that tempers the heat of chillies and complements the richness of coconut milk. Desserts, such as mango sticky rice or coconut-based treats, showcase how sweetness can be celebrated as a standalone flavour, providing a delightful conclusion to a savoury meal.

Salty Savory Depth: Fish sauce, a fundamental ingredient in Thai kitchens, is the cornerstone of saltiness, imparting a savoury depth that enhances the overall flavour profile of a dish. The judicious use of saltiness not only seasons the ingredients but also elevates the umami, creating a savoury experience that is both satisfying and nuanced. Balancing saltiness is an art, ensuring that it complements the other flavours without overpowering them.

Sourness: The infusion of sourness in Thai cuisine comes from a variety of sources, with lime and tamarind being prominent contributors. Whether it's the zesty squeeze of lime over a bowl of noodle soup or the tangy notes of tamarind in a Pad Thai sauce, sourness provides a refreshing and palate-cleansing element. Sourness acts as a bright counterbalance to the richness of coconut milk and the heartiness of meats, creating a dynamic interplay that keeps the taste buds engaged.

Spiciness: Chilies, in various forms, bring the heat that defines the bold and vibrant nature of Thai cuisine. From the mild warmth of a green curry to the fiery kick of a Som Tum salad, spiciness adds a layer of complexity that distinguishes Thai dishes. The degree of heat is often customizable, allowing individuals to tailor their meals to their spice tolerance. Spiciness not only imparts a sensory thrill but also plays a role in the cultural inclination towards "yum," the Thai concept of balance and harmony in flavour.

The Dance of Flavors: In Thai cuisine, achieving the perfect balance of sweet, salty, sour, and spicy is akin to orchestrating a dance of flavours. Each ingredient plays a specific role in this choreography, contributing its unique notes to create a harmonious whole. The balance is not static; it evolves throughout the course of a meal, with each bite inviting the diner to experience a different facet of the flavour spectrum.

Cultural Significance: The emphasis on flavour balance in Thai cuisine is deeply rooted in cultural traditions and the geographical diversity of the country. The abundance of herbs, tropical fruits, and aromatic spices has influenced the development of a culinary approach that celebrates freshness, seasonality, and balance. Thai meals are often communal experiences, where the sharing of dishes allows for a collective exploration of flavour.

Health and Well-Being: Beyond its culinary allure, the balance of flavours in Thai cuisine aligns with principles of holistic health and well-being. The use of fresh herbs, vegetables, and lean proteins contributes to a nutrient-rich diet, while the balance of flavours enhances the overall satisfaction of meals. The interplay of sweet, salty, sour, and spicy elements not only delights the palate but also stimulates digestion, promoting a sense of culinary and physical equilibrium.

Tips for Achieving Balance:

1. **Taste as You Go:** Regular tasting during the cooking process allows for adjustments to the balance of flavours. This hands-on approach ensures that each dish reaches its optimal taste profile.

2. **Understand Ingredient Roles:** Develop an understanding of the flavour profiles of key ingredients. Recognize the role of each

component in contributing sweetness, saltiness, sourness, or spiciness to a dish.

3. **Adapt to Personal Preferences:** Thai cuisine is known for its adaptability. Feel free to adjust the quantity of certain ingredients based on personal taste preferences, whether you prefer a bolder spiciness or a subtler sweetness.

4. **Explore Regional Nuances:** Thai cuisine varies across regions, and each region has its unique approach to balancing flavours. Explore dishes from different regions to appreciate the diverse culinary landscape of Thailand.

5. **Experiment with Herbs and Spices:** Fresh herbs and aromatic spices are key to achieving flavour balance. Experiment with herbs like cilantro, basil, and mint, as well as spices like lemongrass and galangal, to add complexity to your dishes.

Deep dive into the concept of "Yam" - Thai aromatic salads

Embarking on a deep dive into the concept of "Yam," Thai aromatic salads, unveils a world of culinary artistry where freshness, vibrancy, and bold flavours converge in a symphony of taste. "Yam" represents a category of Thai salads that go beyond mere greens, showcasing the country's ingenious ability to elevate humble ingredients into complex, aromatic creations. This exploration delves into the cultural significance, diverse variations, and key elements that define the realm of Thai Yam salads.

Cultural Significance: The concept of Yam extends beyond its literal translation of "salad." It embodies a culinary philosophy that celebrates the balance of flavours and textures, creating a sensory experience that is quintessentially Thai. The word "Yam" is often associated with the concept of "yum," a term that encapsulates the harmonious balance of sweet, sour, salty, and spicy flavours—a fundamental principle in Thai cuisine. Yam salads are emblematic of the country's culinary diversity, with each region contributing its unique variations that reflect local ingredients and preferences.

Key Elements of Yam Salads:

1. **Fresh Herbs:** Yam salads are characterized by an abundance of fresh herbs that contribute aromatic complexity. Cilantro, mint, basil, and coriander are commonly used, infusing the salads with vibrant flavours and fragrances.

2. **Proteins:** Yam salads can feature a variety of proteins, ranging from seafood and poultry to tofu or beef. Grilled, poached, or even raw proteins add a textural element to the salads, making them hearty and satisfying.

3. **Vegetables:** Crisp vegetables play a pivotal role in Yam salads, providing a refreshing

crunch and vibrant colours. Ingredients like cucumbers, tomatoes, red onions, and green beans are often incorporated.

4. **Citrusy Dressings:** The dressings for Yam salads are a vital component, typically crafted with a combination of lime juice, fish sauce, and sometimes tamarind. This citrusy blend imparts a zesty and tangy quality that enhances the overall flavour profile.

5. **Spices and Chilies:** Thai chillies and aromatic spices, such as roasted ground rice or chilli flakes, contribute a layer of heat and depth to Yam salads. The spice level can be adjusted to individual preferences, adding an element of customization to each dish.

Diverse Variations of Yam Salads:

1. **Yam Nua (Beef Salad):** This classic Thai salad features tender slices of grilled beef combined with a medley of fresh herbs, tomatoes, red onions, and a zesty dressing. The marriage of grilled beef and citrusy flavours creates a savoury and refreshing dish.

2. **Yam Pla Dook Foo (Crispy Catfish Salad):** Crispy-fried catfish is the star of this Yam variation. The catfish is shredded into delicate flakes and tossed with green mango, herbs, and a spicy lime dressing, resulting in a texture-rich and flavorful salad.

3. **Yam Wun Sen (Glass Noodle Salad):** Glass noodles, made from mung beans, form the base of this light and refreshing Yam salad. Mixed with shrimp, minced chicken, or tofu, and an assortment of vegetables, the salad is dressed with a lime and fish sauce vinaigrette.

4. **Yam Talay (Seafood Salad):** This seafood-centric Yam brings together an array of fresh seafood, such as squid, shrimp, and mussels, with vibrant herbs and vegetables. The dressing, enriched with lime and fish sauce, complements the brininess of the seafood.

5. **Yam Mamuang (Green Mango Salad):** Green mango, shredded into thin strips, takes centre stage in this Yam variation. The tartness of the green mango is balanced with a sweet and savoury dressing, creating a vibrant and palate-awakening salad.

Culinary Experience: The culinary experience of indulging in a Yam salad is a sensory journey that engages taste, smell, and texture. The vibrant colours of fresh ingredients, the aromatic bouquet of herbs, and the lively interplay of sweet, sour, salty, and spicy flavours create a dish that is as visually appealing as it is delicious. Each bite offers a textural dance of crisp vegetables, tender proteins, and the nuanced crunch of roasted rice or nuts, providing a multisensory delight.

Health Benefits and Freshness: Beyond their delightful flavours, Yam salads align with principles of health and well-being. The emphasis on fresh herbs, vegetables, and lean proteins contributes to a nutrient-rich meal. The citrusy dressings not only enhance flavour but also stimulate digestion, making Yam salads a refreshing and wholesome choice.

Culinary Innovation: While rooted in tradition, Yam salads are also subject to culinary innovation and creativity. Chefs and home cooks alike experiment with variations, introducing new ingredients, proteins, or dressings to create unique interpretations of this Thai classic. This adaptability is a testament to the dynamic nature of Thai cuisine, which continues to evolve while staying true to its core principles.

Tips for Preparing Yam Salads:

1. **Fresh Ingredients:** Use the freshest herbs, vegetables, and proteins available. The quality of ingredients is paramount in Yam salads, as their vibrancy contributes to the overall sensory experience.

2. **Balance of Flavors:** Pay careful attention to achieving a balance of sweet, sour, salty, and spicy flavours in the dressing. Taste as you go and adjust the quantities to suit your preferences.

3. **Texture Matters:** Incorporate a variety of textures by including crisp vegetables, tender proteins, and crunchy elements like roasted rice or nuts. This adds complexity and excitement to each bite.

4. **Customization:** Feel free to customize Yam salads based on personal preferences.

Experiment with proteins, vegetables, or herbs to create your unique version of this Thai culinary gem.

5. **Presentation:** Yam salads are not only delicious but also visually striking. Pay attention to the presentation, arranging ingredients thoughtfully to showcase the vibrant colours and textures.

Recipe: "Laab Gai" - Spicy chicken salad

Embarking on the culinary journey of "Laab Gai," a spicy chicken salad from Thailand, unveils a vibrant tapestry of flavours that exemplifies the bold and aromatic nature of Thai cuisine. This dish, hailing from the northeastern region of Thailand, is a harmonious blend of minced chicken, fresh herbs, and an assertive mix of spices. As we delve into the steps of preparing Laab Gai, we unravel the culinary secrets that make this spicy chicken salad a favourite for those seeking an adventure in taste.

Ingredients:

1. **Ground Chicken:** Use lean ground chicken to ensure a tender and flavorful base for the salad.

2. **Shallots:** Finely minced shallots contribute a sweet and mild onion flavour to the dish.

3. **Lime:** Fresh lime juice provides a zesty and citrusy kick that brightens the overall flavour profile.

4. **Fish Sauce:** A key component in Thai cuisine, fish sauce adds depth, umami, and saltiness to Laab Gai.

5. **Roasted Rice Powder:** Coarsely ground roasted rice adds a nutty and crunchy texture, enhancing the overall mouthfeel of the salad.

6. **Thai Bird's Eye Chilies:** These small but potent chillies bring the heat to Laab Gai. Adjust the quantity based on your spice preferences.

7. **Fresh Herbs (Cilantro, Mint, Thai Basil):** A combination of fresh herbs adds aromatic complexity and freshness to the salad.

8. **Green Onions:** Finely chopped green onions contribute a mild onion flavour and a subtle crunch.

9. **Lettuce Leaves:** Lettuce leaves serve as a vessel for the Laab Gai, offering a refreshing contrast to the bold flavours.

Cooking Process:

1. **Cook the Ground Chicken:** In a skillet over medium heat, cook the ground chicken until fully browned and cooked through. Break it apart with a spatula to achieve a fine, crumbly texture.

2. **Prepare the Dressing:** In a bowl, combine lime juice and fish sauce. Adjust the ratio to achieve a balance of tartness and saltiness. Add finely chopped Thai bird's eye chillies for

spiciness. Taste and adjust the dressing according to your preference.

3. **Toast and Grind the Rice:** In a dry pan, toast uncooked rice until golden brown. Once toasted, grind the rice into a coarse powder using a mortar and pestle or a spice grinder. This roasted rice powder will add a delightful crunch to the Laab Gai.

4. **Combine Ingredients:** In a large mixing bowl, combine the cooked ground chicken, minced shallots, chopped green onions, and roasted rice powder. Mix these ingredients thoroughly.

5. **Add Fresh Herbs:** Incorporate the fresh herbs—cilantro, mint, and Thai basil—into the bowl. The herbs contribute a burst of aromatic freshness to the salad.

6. **Pour in Dressing:** Pour the lime juice and fish sauce dressing over the mixture. Toss the salad gently, ensuring that the dressing evenly coats the ingredients.

7. **Taste and Adjust:** Taste the Laab Gai and adjust the seasoning as needed. You can add more lime juice, fish sauce, or chillies according to your taste preferences.

8. **Serve with Lettuce Leaves:** Arrange lettuce leaves on a serving platter. Spoon the Laab Gai mixture onto the leaves, creating individual wraps. The lettuce acts as a cool

and crisp vessel that complements the heat and bold flavours of the salad.

Culinary Experience:

Laab Gai offers a culinary experience that engages the senses with each bite. The combination of tender ground chicken, aromatic herbs, the crunch of roasted rice, and the spicy kick from Thai bird's eye chillies creates a symphony of flavours that dance on the palate. The freshness of lime and the savoury depth of fish sauce add layers of complexity, making Laab Gai a dish that is both bold and refreshing.

Customization and Variations:

1. **Protein Options:** While Laab Gai traditionally features ground chicken, you can explore variations with other proteins such as pork, beef, or even tofu for a vegetarian option.

2. **Spice Level:** Adjust the spice level to suit your taste preferences. If you enjoy intense heat, increase the quantity of Thai bird's eye chillies, or conversely, reduce them for a milder version.

3. **Herb Choices:** Experiment with the herb combination based on your preferences. Some variations of Laab Gai include additional herbs like sawtooth coriander or culantro for added depth.

4. **Vegetables:** Enhance the nutritional content and texture by adding finely chopped vegetables such as cucumber, cherry tomatoes, or red bell peppers to the salad.

Cultural Significance:

Laab Gai is deeply rooted in the culinary traditions of Thailand, particularly in the northeastern region known as Isaan. The dish is a staple at gatherings, celebrations, and family meals. Its popularity stems from its ability to showcase the bold and aromatic flavours that define Thai cuisine, making it a beloved dish both within the country and on the global culinary stage.

Health Benefits:

Beyond its delectable taste, Laab Gai aligns with the principles of healthy eating. The lean protein from ground chicken, coupled with fresh herbs and minimal oil, makes it a nutritious choice. The inclusion of lime juice not only enhances flavour but also provides a dose of vitamin C.

Presentation Tips:

1. **Colorful Arrangement:** Arrange the Laab Gai mixture on a platter with an emphasis on colour and visual appeal. The vibrant greens of herbs and the golden-brown roasted rice create an enticing presentation.

2. **Lettuce Cups:** Serve Laab Gai with fresh lettuce leaves on the side. This allows diners

to create individual wraps, adding an
interactive element to the meal.

3. **Garnish:** Garnish the Laab Gai with
    additional herb leaves, a sprinkle of roasted
    rice powder, and thin slices of lime for a
    finishing touch.

Chapter 5: "Delights from the Thai Sea"

Exploration of seafood and fresh fish-based cuisine

Embarking on an exploration of seafood and fresh
fish-based cuisine unveils a world of culinary delights
that reflects the coastal richness and vibrant diversity
of flavours. From the bustling markets of Thailand to
seaside eateries around the globe, the use of seafood
in culinary traditions represents a celebration of the
ocean's bounty. This culinary journey encompasses a
myriad of dishes that highlight the exquisite

freshness, delicate textures, and nuanced flavours of seafood, creating an experience that resonates with both coastal communities and lovers of fine cuisine worldwide.

Cultural Significance: Seafood has long held cultural significance in coastal regions, shaping culinary traditions and community identities. The reliance on fresh fish and seafood is not merely a matter of sustenance; it is a reflection of the deep connection between communities and their maritime environments. This relationship is often celebrated through seafood festivals, traditional fishing methods, and recipes that have been passed down through generations.

Diverse Culinary Techniques: The exploration of seafood-based cuisine encompasses a wide range of culinary techniques, from simple grilling and steaming to complex preparations that showcase the artistry of seafood culinary traditions. Each region around the world has its own approach, influenced by local ingredients, cultural practices, and the unique marine life found in its waters.

Sushi and Sashimi in Japanese Cuisine: Japanese cuisine is renowned for its meticulous preparation of sushi and sashimi, showcasing the purity and freshness of seafood. Sushi involves vinegared rice combined with a variety of ingredients, including raw or cooked seafood, while sashimi focuses on thinly sliced raw fish, often served with soy sauce and wasabi. The artistry in presentation and the emphasis on simplicity allow the natural flavours of the seafood to shine.

Mediterranean Grilled Seafood: Mediterranean cuisine, with its emphasis on olive oil, fresh herbs, and bold flavours, celebrates the simplicity of grilled seafood. Whole fish, shrimp, calamari, and octopus are often marinated, seasoned, and grilled to perfection. The result is a dish that captures the essence of the sea while allowing the natural flavours of the seafood to be enhanced by the smokiness of the grill.

Thai Tom Yum Soup: Thailand's culinary landscape features a vibrant array of seafood dishes, and Tom Yum Soup stands out as a spicy and sour masterpiece. Packed with ingredients like shrimp, squid, mussels, and fish, this aromatic soup is infused with lemongrass, kaffir lime leaves, and Thai bird's eye chillies. The combination of bold flavours and diverse textures makes Tom Yum Soup a culinary adventure that exemplifies the dynamic nature of Thai seafood cuisine.

Peruvian Ceviche: In Peru, ceviche is a beloved dish that transforms fresh fish and seafood into a refreshing and zesty delight. Raw fish is cured in citrus juices, typically lime or lemon, and then mixed with onions, chilli peppers, cilantro, and other seasonings. The result is a dish that encapsulates the brightness of the ocean and the boldness of Peruvian flavours.

The Art of Seafood Paella in Spain: Spain's culinary heritage boasts the iconic seafood paella, a rice dish infused with an assortment of seafood such as prawns, mussels, clams, and squid. The dish is enriched with saffron, paprika, and a flavorful broth, creating a symphony of tastes and aromas. Seafood paella reflects the cultural diversity of Spain's coastal regions and the influence of the Mediterranean on its culinary traditions.

Health Benefits and Nutritional Richness: Seafood is renowned for its nutritional richness, providing an abundant source of lean proteins, omega-3 fatty acids, vitamins, and minerals. The consumption of seafood has been linked to various health benefits, including heart health, brain function, and overall well-being. The low levels of saturated fats in most seafood make it a nutritious option that aligns with modern dietary preferences.

Sustainability and Responsible Fishing Practices: As the global demand for seafood continues to rise, there is a growing emphasis on sustainability and responsible fishing practices. Many culinary communities and chefs are championing sustainable seafood sourcing to ensure the health of marine ecosystems and the livelihoods of fishing communities. The "sea-to-table" movement promotes transparency in the seafood supply chain, allowing consumers to make informed choices about the environmental impact of their seafood consumption.

Culinary Innovation and Fusion: The exploration of seafood cuisine is not confined to traditional recipes; it also encompasses culinary innovation and fusion. Chefs around the world are pushing the boundaries, combining global influences and inventive techniques to create dishes that are both rooted in tradition and boldly contemporary. Seafood tacos with Asian-inspired slaw, lobster sushi rolls, or ceviche with tropical fruit infusions are examples of how culinary boundaries are continually evolving.

Cooking Tips for Seafood Enthusiasts:

1. **Freshness is Key:** When working with seafood, prioritizing freshness is paramount. Look for clear, vibrant eyes in whole fish, firm flesh in fillets, and a fresh, briny aroma.

2. **Appreciate Seasonality:** Seafood, like other ingredients, has seasons. Be mindful of the seasonal availability of specific types of seafood to ensure the best quality and flavour.

3. **Adapt Recipes to Local Ingredients:** Embrace the diversity of local seafood options. Adapt global seafood recipes to include locally available fish and shellfish, adding a regional twist to your dishes.

4. **Experiment with Different Cooking Techniques:** Explore various cooking methods, from grilling and baking to steaming and ceviche-style preparations. Each technique accentuates different aspects of seafood's natural flavours and textures.

5. **Pairing with Complementary Flavors:** Experiment with flavour pairings that complement the natural taste of seafood. Citrus, herbs, garlic, and aromatic spices can enhance the overall culinary experience.

Introduction to dishes like "Pla Rad Prik" - fried fish with spicy sauce

Introducing dishes like "Pla Rad Prik" brings us into the heart of Thai culinary excellence, where bold flavours, vibrant ingredients, and expert techniques come together to create a gastronomic symphony. Pla Rad Prik, which translates to "fried fish with spicy sauce," is a Thai culinary masterpiece that exemplifies the country's prowess in balancing heat, sweetness, and umami. As we delve into the introduction of this delectable dish, we uncover the cultural significance, key components, and culinary artistry that make Pla Rad Prik a standout in Thai cuisine.

Cultural Significance: Pla Rad Prik embodies the rich culinary heritage of Thailand, reflecting the country's deep connection to its abundant aquatic resources. Thailand's geography, surrounded by seas and boasting numerous rivers, has bestowed upon its cuisine an array of fresh and diverse seafood. Fish, a staple in Thai culinary traditions, takes centre stage in Pla Rad Prik, showcasing how the vibrant flavours of Thai cuisine are intertwined with the bounties of the land and sea.

Key Components of Pla Rad Prik:

1. **Fish:** The choice of fish is crucial in Pla Rad Prik. Whole fish, often with crispy skin achieved through deep-frying, is favoured for its succulent and tender flesh. Varieties such as snapper or tilapia are commonly used, and

the presentation of a whole fish adds visual appeal to the dish.

2. **Spicy Sauce (Prik Nam Pla):** The spicy sauce, known as Prik Nam Pla, is the soul of Pla Rad Prik. This sauce typically consists of Thai bird's eye chillies, garlic, lime juice, fish sauce, and a touch of sweetness. The sauce's bold and piquant nature complements the delicate flavour of the fried fish, creating a harmonious balance.

3. **Herbs and Garnishes:** Pla Rad Prik often features a medley of fresh herbs and aromatics such as cilantro, mint, and green onions. These additions contribute brightness, freshness, and an additional layer of flavour to the dish.

4. **Deep-Frying Technique:** The deep-frying technique used in Pla Rad Prik achieves a crispy and golden exterior while maintaining the juiciness of the fish inside. This method not only enhances the texture of the fish but also provides a canvas for the spicy sauce to cling to, ensuring each bite is a delightful crunch of flavour.

Culinary Artistry: The preparation of Pla Rad Prik requires a finesse that Thai chefs have mastered over generations. The artistry lies in the meticulous balance of flavours, where the heat from the spicy sauce harmonizes with the natural sweetness of the fish. The presentation, often featuring a whole fish adorned with vibrant herbs, is a testament to the aesthetic considerations that are integral to Thai culinary culture.

Flavour Dynamics: Pla Rad Prik encapsulates the four fundamental flavours of Thai cuisine – sweet, sour, salty, and spicy. The crispy fish serves as a canvas for the vibrant and aromatic Prik Nam Pla, which combines the heat of chillies, the tanginess of lime, and the savoury depth of fish sauce. The interplay of these flavours creates a multidimensional taste experience that is both invigorating and satisfying.

Customization and Regional Variations: While Pla Rad Prik has its classic components, the dish is subject to regional variations and personal preferences. In some versions, chefs may add a touch of sweetness with palm sugar or balance the heat with additional lime juice. Regional adaptations may incorporate local herbs or spices, showcasing the diversity within Thai cuisine.

Culinary Experience: Indulging in Pla Rad Prik is a culinary experience that engages the senses at multiple levels. The sight of a beautifully presented whole fish, the aroma of crispy perfection, and the first bite into the succulent flesh followed by the explosive flavours of the spicy sauce create a memorable journey. Each element, from the crispy exterior to the aromatic sauce, contributes to a dining experience that is both satisfying and evocative of the vibrant Thai culinary spirit.

Tips for Enjoying Pla Rad Prik:

1. **Freshness Matters:** Opt for the freshest fish available. The quality of the fish is fundamental to achieving the desired texture and flavour.

2. **Spice Level Customization:** Thai cuisine often allows for the customization of spice levels. Adjust the quantity of Thai bird's eye chillies in the Prik Nam Pla to match your preferred level of heat.

3. **Accompaniments:** Pla Rad Prik is often served with a side of steamed jasmine rice to soak up the flavorful sauce. The combination of the crispy fish and aromatic rice is a perfect marriage of textures.

4. **Explore Variations:** Experiment with different types of fish or regional variations of Pla Rad Prik. Each variation offers a unique twist on the classic dish.

Culinary Heritage and Global Influence: As a representative dish of Thai cuisine, Pla Rad Prik has not only captivated local palates but has also gained international acclaim. Thai restaurants around the world feature this dish, allowing global audiences to savour the authentic flavours of Thailand. Pla Rad Prik's influence extends beyond the plate, becoming a symbol of Thai culinary artistry and the harmonious marriage of bold and nuanced flavours.

Recipe: "Tom Kha Talay" - Seafood coconut soup

Embarking on the culinary adventure of preparing "Tom Kha Talay," a luscious seafood coconut soup from Thailand, promises a journey into the heart of Thai flavours—a harmonious blend of creamy coconut, aromatic herbs, and the briny essence of the sea. This beloved Thai dish is a testament to the country's culinary mastery, where each ingredient plays a role in creating a symphony of tastes that dance on the palate. As we delve into the recipe for Tom Kha Talay, we explore the key components, cooking techniques, and cultural significance that make this seafood coconut soup a cherished gem in Thai gastronomy.

Ingredients:

1. **Assorted Seafood:** Tom Kha Talay typically features a mix of seafood, such as shrimp, mussels, squid, and fish. The variety contributes to the depth and complexity of flavours.

2. **Coconut Milk:** The creamy base of Tom Kha Talay comes from rich coconut milk. It adds a luxurious texture and imparts a subtle sweetness to the soup.

3. **Galangal:** A rhizome similar to ginger, galangal is a key ingredient that infuses Tom Kha Talay with its distinct citrusy and earthy flavour.

4. **Lemongrass:** Fragrant lemongrass adds a zesty and citrusy note to the soup, enhancing its overall aroma and taste.

5. **Kaffir Lime Leaves:** These aromatic leaves contribute a unique citrusy and floral flavour, enhancing the Thai character of the soup.

6. **Thai Bird's Eye Chilies:** For a touch of heat, Thai bird's eye chillies are added. The quantity can be adjusted based on personal spice preferences.

7. **Mushrooms:** Sliced mushrooms, such as straw mushrooms or shiitake, provide additional texture and absorb the flavours of the broth.

8. **Fish Sauce:** A fundamental ingredient in Thai cuisine, the fish sauce adds saltiness and umami, enhancing the overall savoury profile of the soup.

9. **Lime Juice:** Fresh lime juice adds a tangy and refreshing element to balance the richness of the coconut milk.

10. **Cilantro:** Fresh cilantro leaves, added as a garnish, contribute a burst of freshness and herbaceous aroma.

Cooking Process:

1. **Prepare the Ingredients:** Clean and devein the shrimp, slice the squid into rings, and cut the fish into bite-sized pieces. Prepare galangal by peeling and thinly slicing it.

Bruise the lemongrass stalks to release their flavour. Tear the kaffir lime leaves into pieces.

2. **Simmer the Broth:** In a pot, bring coconut milk to a gentle simmer over medium heat. Add galangal, lemongrass, and kaffir lime leaves. Allow the broth to infuse with these aromatic ingredients for 5-7 minutes.

3. **Add Seafood and Vegetables:** Introduce the assorted seafood and sliced mushrooms into the simmering broth. Cook until the seafood is just opaque and cooked through, ensuring it remains tender.

4. **Season the Soup:** Season the soup with fish sauce for saltiness and lime juice for acidity. Adjust the quantities to achieve a balance of flavours, keeping in mind the preference for sweetness, saltiness, and tanginess.

5. **Adjust Spice Level:** Add Thai bird's eye chillies according to the desired spice level. Be cautious, as these chillies can be quite potent.

6. **Serve Hot:** Once the seafood is cooked, remove the soup from the heat. Discard lemongrass stalks and kaffir lime leaves. Ladle the Tom Kha Talay into serving bowls.

7. **Garnish with Cilantro:** Finish the soup by garnishing it with fresh cilantro leaves. The cilantro adds a final touch of brightness to the dish.

Culinary Experience:

Tom Kha Talay offers a culinary experience that engages the senses with its velvety texture, aromatic fragrance, and dynamic flavours. The richness of coconut milk provides a luxurious backdrop for the vibrant interplay of seafood, citrusy lemongrass, and the earthy warmth of galangal. Each spoonful unveils a medley of tastes—sweetness from coconut, umami from fish sauce, a hint of spice from chillies, and the refreshing acidity of lime juice.

Customization and Variations:

1. **Vegetarian Option:** For a vegetarian version, omit the seafood and opt for a mix of mushrooms and tofu. The soup's aromatic base pairs beautifully with a variety of vegetables.

2. **Protein Choices:** Experiment with different combinations of seafood, choosing varieties that are fresh and readily available. Consider incorporating crab, clams, or even lobster for a luxurious twist.

3. **Herb Infusions:** Enhance the herbal complexity by adding Thai basil or additional herbs like coriander to the soup. These herbs contribute unique aromatic profiles, elevating the overall experience.

4. **Spice Spectrum:** Tailor the spice level to personal preferences. Adjust the quantity of Thai bird's eye chillies or incorporate milder chillies for those who prefer less heat.

Health Benefits:

Beyond its enticing flavours, Tom Kha Talay offers health benefits rooted in its fresh and wholesome ingredients. Seafood provides lean proteins and essential omega-3 fatty acids, while coconut milk adds richness and provides healthy fats. The infusion of herbs and spices contributes antioxidants and anti-inflammatory properties, making this soup a nourishing choice.

Cultural Significance:

Tom Kha Talay is deeply ingrained in Thai culinary traditions and holds cultural significance as a comforting and celebratory dish. Often enjoyed as part of festive gatherings or family meals, the soup embodies the warmth of Thai hospitality and the country's reverence for fresh, high-quality ingredients.

Presentation Tips:

1. **Bowl Arrangement:** Serve Tom Kha Talay in individual bowls, allowing the vibrant colours of seafood and herbs to shine through. The contrast of white coconut milk and assorted seafood creates an aesthetically pleasing presentation.

2. **Herb Garnish:** Arrange cilantro leaves on top of the soup just before serving. The bright green herbs add visual appeal and a burst of freshness.

3. **Lime Wedges:** Place lime wedges on the side for diners to squeeze into their soup, allowing for a customizable level of acidity.

Chapter 6: "Northern Flavors vs. Southern Flavors"

Analysis of culinary differences between the northern and southern regions of Thailand

The culinary landscape of Thailand is a vibrant tapestry woven with diverse flavours, ingredients, and cooking techniques that vary significantly between its northern and southern regions. This culinary divergence reflects the rich cultural, geographical, and historical influences that have shaped the distinct gastronomic identities of Northern and Southern Thai cuisines.

Northern Thai Cuisine:

Flavours and Influences: Northern Thai cuisine, often referred to as Lanna cuisine, is characterized by bold, earthy flavours and a penchant for savoury, herbal, and aromatic profiles. The region's cuisine draws inspiration from the mountainous terrain, cooler climate, and historical connections with neighbouring countries like Myanmar and Laos.

Key Ingredients:

1. **Sticky Rice:** A staple in Northern Thailand, sticky rice serves as the foundation of many meals. Its unique texture complements the bold flavours of Northern dishes.

2. **Herbs and Aromatics:** The use of fragrant herbs such as basil, mint, and cilantro is prominent. Northern Thai dishes often feature a variety of aromatic spices like galangal, turmeric, and cardamom.

3. **Proteins:** Due to the region's topography, Northern Thai cuisine incorporates game meats, such as boar and venison, as well as freshwater fish. Pork is a favoured protein, showcased in dishes like "Khao Soi," a coconut-based curry noodle soup.

Signature Dishes:

1. **Khao Soi:** This iconic dish is a fragrant and rich coconut curry soup served with both crispy and boiled egg noodles, topped with pickled mustard greens, shallots, lime, and ground chillies.

2. **Nam Prik Ong:** A savoury pork and tomato chilli dip, typically served with an array of fresh vegetables and sticky rice.

3. **Larb Moo:** A minced pork salad seasoned with lime, fish sauce, and an assortment of herbs, offering a perfect blend of tangy and savoury flavours.

Southern Thai Cuisine:

Flavours and Influences: Southern Thai cuisine, with its bold and fiery flavours, is a culinary expedition into the tropical coastal regions. The proximity to the sea, along with influences from Malaysia and Indonesia, contributes to the intense spiciness and the inclusion of coconut-based dishes.

Key Ingredients:

1. **Coconut Milk:** An integral part of Southern Thai cuisine, coconut milk lends richness to many dishes, creating a creamy and flavorful base.

2. **Chilies:** Southern Thai cuisine is renowned for its fiery dishes, often incorporating a variety of chillies to intensify the heat.

3. **Seafood:** With its expansive coastline, Southern Thailand boasts an abundance of fresh seafood. Shrimp, crab, and various fish varieties play a central role in Southern dishes.

Signature Dishes:

1. **Gaeng Tai Pla:** A piquant and aromatic fish curry, featuring a mix of herbs, spices, and fermented shrimp paste.

2. **Pad Ped:** A stir-fry dish bursting with flavours, often made with fish or shrimp and featuring an aromatic blend of curry paste, kaffir lime leaves, and Thai basil.

3. **Tom Yam:** While Tom Yam is enjoyed across Thailand, the Southern version often features a spicier and more intense broth, packed with fresh herbs, lemongrass, and lime.

Contrasts and Commonalities:

1. Spice Levels:

- **Northern Cuisine:** While Northern Thai cuisine can be flavorful and aromatic, it tends to be milder in terms of spice compared to its Southern counterpart.

- **Southern Cuisine:** The use of chillies is more assertive in Southern Thai cuisine, resulting in dishes that are known for their intense heat and bold flavours.

2. Ingredient Utilization:

- **Northern Cuisine:** Fresh herbs and game meats are prevalent in Northern Thai dishes. The cuisine celebrates the use of locally sourced ingredients, reflecting the region's agricultural abundance.

- **Southern Cuisine:** Coconut milk, fresh seafood, and a potent mix of chillies and spices are the stars of Southern Thai cuisine. The coastal influence is evident in the emphasis on seafood-centric dishes.

3. Influences from Neighboring Countries:

- **Northern Cuisine:** Influences from neighbouring Myanmar and Laos are notable, shaping the character of Northern Thai dishes with distinct herbal and savoury notes.

- **Southern Cuisine:** Proximity to Malaysia and Indonesia has influenced Southern Thai cuisine, contributing to the use of coconut milk and a spicier flavour profile.

4. Rice Varieties:

- **Northern Cuisine:** Sticky rice is a staple, providing a chewy texture that complements the savoury dishes.

- **Southern Cuisine:** Jasmine rice is commonly used in Southern Thailand, offering a fragrant and light accompaniment to the robust flavours of the cuisine.

Culinary Harmony:

While Northern and Southern Thai cuisines showcase distinct characteristics, it's essential to recognize the overarching culinary principles that unite Thai gastronomy. Both regions share a reverence for fresh, aromatic herbs, a balance of flavours encompassing sweet, salty, sour, and spicy, and a commitment to using locally sourced ingredients. Rice, in its various forms, remains a fundamental element that ties together the diverse culinary traditions of Thailand.

Regional Diversity in Thai Cuisine:

The culinary diversity between Northern and Southern Thailand is just one facet of the broader tapestry of Thai gastronomy. Central and northeastern regions each contribute their unique flavours and culinary traditions, further enriching the multifaceted nature of Thai cuisine. Exploring the regional nuances allows for a deeper appreciation of the cultural, geographical, and historical influences that have shaped the culinary landscape of this vibrant and captivating Southeast Asian nation.

Presentation of typical dishes from the North and the South

The presentation of typical dishes from the North and the South of Thailand is a visual feast that reflects the diverse culinary traditions, cultural influences, and geographical nuances of each region. As we explore the distinctive elements of these presentations, it becomes evident that beyond the vibrant flavours, Thai cuisine is an art form that engages the senses through meticulous attention to aesthetics, balance, and the celebration of fresh, locally sourced ingredients.

Northern Thai Dishes:

1. **Khao Soi:**

   - **Visual Elements:** Khao Soi, a signature dish of Northern Thailand, is a captivating visual delight. The dish is typically presented with a vibrant contrast of golden-yellow curry broth, both crispy and boiled egg noodles, and an array of colourful toppings.

   - **Garnishes:** The toppings include fresh cilantro, shallots, pickled mustard greens, lime wedges, and crispy fried noodles. This meticulous arrangement not only adds visual appeal but also enhances the overall flavour profile.

2. **Nam Prik Ong:**

- **Plating Style:** Nam Prik Ong, a savoury pork and tomato chilli dip, is presented in a communal style, often served in a central bowl surrounded by an assortment of fresh vegetables.

- **Color Palette:** The dish showcases a spectrum of colours, from the vibrant red of the chilli dip to the greenery of cucumber, Thai eggplant, and long beans. This visually inviting presentation encourages communal dining and sharing.

3. **Larb Moo:**

- **Plate Composition:** Larb Moo, a minced pork salad, is elegantly presented on a plate, allowing the vibrant colours of the ingredients to shine through.

- **Herb Accents:** Fresh herbs like mint and cilantro are strategically placed as accents, adding a burst of greenery to the dish. The aromatic herbs not only enhance the visual appeal but also contribute to the overall freshness of the presentation.

Southern Thai Dishes:

1. **Gaeng Tai Pla:**

   - **Bowl Presentation:** Gaeng Tai Pla, a piquant fish curry, is traditionally served in a bowl, allowing the rich and aromatic broth to take centre stage.

   - **Layered Appearance:** The soup often features layers of ingredients, including fish, herbs, and vegetables, creating a visually intricate and appetizing presentation. The deep reddish-brown colour of the broth adds to the visual allure.

2. **Pad Ped:**

   - **Wok Showcase:** Pad Ped, a spicy stir-fry dish, is frequently presented in a wok or a shallow pan, showcasing the sizzling and vibrant cooking process.

   - **Vegetable Medley:** The dish incorporates a colourful medley of vegetables, adding visual interest and nutritional variety. The glossy appearance of the stir-fry highlights the skilful combination of sauces and spices.

3. **Tom Yam:**

   - **Transparent Elegance:** Tom Yam, a hot and sour soup, is often served in clear bowls, allowing the colourful

and aromatic broth to be fully
appreciated.

- **Floating Ingredients:** The soup
  showcases ingredients like shrimp,
  mushrooms, and vibrant herbs
  floating in the translucent broth. This
  presentation not only emphasizes
  freshness but also invites diners to
  savour the visual and aromatic
  aspects of the dish before indulging in
  its flavours.

Commonalities in Presentation:

1. **Herb and Garnish Emphasis:**

   - **Northern and Southern Cuisine:**
     Both regions place a strong emphasis
     on the use of fresh herbs and
     garnishes. Whether it's the aromatic
     mint in Larb Moo or the cilantro in
     Khao Soi, herbs contribute not only to
     the flavour but also to the visual
     appeal of the dishes.

2. **Colorful Vegetable Accents:**

   - **Northern and Southern Cuisine:**
     The use of vibrant and colourful
     vegetables is a shared characteristic.
     Whether it's the pickled mustard
     greens in Khao Soi or the array of
     fresh vegetables in Nam Prik Ong, the
     inclusion of colourful elements
     enhances the overall presentation.

3. **Communal Dining Presentation:**

- **Northern and Southern Cuisine:**
  Both regions often present dishes in a communal style, encouraging shared dining experiences. This communal aspect reflects the social and convivial nature of Thai meals, where family and friends come together to enjoy a variety of flavours.

Culinary Artistry in Presentation:

Thai cuisine, in both the North and the South, demonstrates culinary artistry not just in the preparation of flavours but also in the thoughtful presentation of dishes. The careful arrangement of ingredients, the use of contrasting colours and textures, and the incorporation of visual elements like fresh herbs and garnishes elevate the dining experience beyond taste alone. The artful presentation serves as a testament to the cultural pride, creativity, and attention to detail embedded in Thai culinary traditions.

Harmony in Diversity:

While the presentation of typical dishes from the North and the South showcases distinct regional characteristics, it's essential to recognize the harmonious aspects that unite these culinary traditions. The use of fresh, locally sourced ingredients, the emphasis on balance in flavours, and the celebration of communal dining are threads that run through the tapestry of Thai cuisine, connecting diverse regions into a rich and cohesive culinary heritage.

Northern Recipe: "Khao Soi" - Curry noodle soup. Delving into the culinary treasures of Northern Thailand, the iconic dish that takes centre stage is "Khao Soi," a soul-warming curry noodle soup that encapsulates the essence of Northern Thai flavours. From its rich and aromatic coconut-based broth to the contrast of crispy and boiled egg noodles, Khao Soi is a culinary masterpiece that invites the palate on a journey through the intricate tapestry of Thai gastronomy.

Ingredients:

1. **Chicken or Beef:** Khao Soi can be prepared with either succulent chicken pieces or tender beef, providing flexibility to suit different preferences.

2. **Egg Noodles:** The dish features a combination of crispy deep-fried egg noodles, adding a delightful crunch, and soft, boiled egg noodles that soak up the flavours of the broth.

3. **Coconut Milk:** The velvety richness of coconut milk forms the luscious base of the curry broth, contributing a creamy texture and a hint of sweetness.

4. **Curry Paste:** A fragrant and aromatic curry paste, made with a blend of spices like

coriander, turmeric, and Thai chillies, infuses the broth with depth and complexity.

5. **Fresh Herbs:** A medley of fresh herbs, including cilantro and green onions, adds brightness and a burst of herbal aroma to the dish.

6. **Shallots:** Sliced shallots are often used as a garnish, providing a mild oniony flavour and a textural contrast.

7. **Lime Wedges:** Served on the side, lime wedges offer a tangy element, allowing diners to customize the acidity of their soup.

Cooking Process:

1. **Prepare the Curry Paste:**
   - Begin by preparing the curry paste, combining ground coriander, turmeric, Thai chillies, and other aromatic spices. This paste forms the foundation of the rich and flavorful broth.

2. **Cooking the Protein:**
   - If using chicken or beef, cook the meat in the curry paste until it's fully coated and infused with the spices. This initial step ensures that the protein absorbs the essence of the curry.

3. **Adding Coconut Milk:**

- Introduce coconut milk to the pot, creating a velvety and aromatic base for the soup. The coconut milk contributes a luxurious creaminess that balances the heat from the curry paste.

4. **Simmering the Broth:**

    - Allow the broth to simmer, allowing the flavours to meld and intensify. The fragrance of the spices, combined with the richness of coconut milk, permeates the kitchen, creating an enticing aroma.

5. **Preparing the Noodles:**

    - While the broth simmers, cook both the crispy and boiled egg noodles separately. The crispy noodles are achieved by deep-frying, providing a delightful crunch to the dish.

6. **Assembly:**

    - To serve Khao Soi, arrange a nest of both crispy and boiled noodles in a bowl. Ladle the fragrant curry broth over the noodles, ensuring that the protein is generously distributed.

7. **Garnishing:**

    - Garnish the dish with fresh cilantro, sliced green onions, and shallots. The addition of these herbs elevates the visual appeal and imparts a burst of freshness.

8. **Accompaniments:**

   - Serve lime wedges on the side, allowing diners to squeeze fresh lime juice into their soup. This step adds a customizable tanginess that enhances the overall flavour profile.

Culinary Experience:

Khao Soi offers a multisensory culinary experience that begins with the enticing aroma wafting from the pot. The first spoonful reveals a symphony of flavours—creamy coconut, fragrant spices, and tender bites of protein. The textural interplay between the crispy and boiled noodles adds depth, creating a satisfying and comforting bowl of soup.

Customization and Variations:

1. **Protein Choices:**

   - While chicken and beef are common choices, Khao Soi can be customized with other proteins, such as tofu or shrimp, catering to diverse dietary preferences.

2. **Spice Level:**

   - Adjust the spice level by varying the number of Thai chillies in the curry paste. This customization allows individuals to tailor the heat to their taste.

3. **Vegetarian Version:**
    - For a vegetarian version, omitting the meat and incorporating a variety of vegetables provides a wholesome and flavorful alternative.

Cultural Significance:

Khao Soi holds cultural significance in Northern Thailand, where it is not just a meal but a symbol of communal dining and shared moments. Often enjoyed in lively markets or family gatherings, this dish reflects the warmth and hospitality embedded in Northern Thai culinary traditions.

Presentation Tips:

1. **Bowl Arrangement:**
    - Serve Khao Soi in individual bowls, ensuring that the contrasting noodles and vibrant broth create an enticing visual display.

2. **Herb Placement:**
    - Garnish the dish with fresh herbs just before serving, allowing the greenery to pop against the golden hues of the curry broth.

3. **Accompaniments Placement:**

- Arrange lime wedges on the side or on a separate plate, inviting diners to engage in the interactive process of customizing the soup to their liking.

Global Appreciation:

Beyond the borders of Thailand, Khao Soi has gained international acclaim, captivating the palates of food enthusiasts worldwide. Thai restaurants around the globe feature this dish, offering a taste of Northern Thailand's culinary excellence and the harmonious blend of flavours that define Khao Soi.

Southern Recipe: "Gaeng Som Pla" - Sour fish curry

Embarking on a culinary expedition into Southern Thailand, one encounters the vibrant and tantalizing "Gaeng Som Pla," a sour fish curry that embodies the bold and fiery flavours of the region. This iconic dish is a testament to the Southern Thai culinary heritage, where the interplay of sourness, spiciness, and aromatic herbs creates a symphony of tastes that captivates the palate. As we delve into the recipe for Gaeng Som Pla, we unravel the secrets behind its preparation, the key ingredients that define its character, and the cultural significance that makes it a culinary treasure in Southern Thai cuisine.

Ingredients:

1. **Assorted Fish:** Gaeng Som Pla traditionally features a variety of fresh fish, such as

snapper or mackerel, adding a briny and savoury dimension to the curry.

2. **Tamarind Paste:** The distinctive sourness of Gaeng Som Pla comes from tamarind paste, a key ingredient that contributes a tangy and citrusy flavour.

3. **Shrimp Paste:** A small amount of shrimp paste is used to enhance the umami depth of the curry, adding a savoury and robust undertone.

4. **Chilies:** Thai bird's eye chillies are a crucial element, providing the characteristic heat that defines Southern Thai cuisine. The quantity can be adjusted to suit individual spice preferences.

5. **Lemongrass:** Fragrant lemongrass imparts a citrusy aroma, infusing the curry with a refreshing and herbal note.

6. **Galangal:** A rhizome similar to ginger, galangal adds a unique warmth and depth to the curry, contributing to its complex flavour profile.

7. **Kaffir Lime Leaves:** These aromatic leaves lend a citrusy and floral fragrance to Gaeng Som Pla, enhancing the overall aromatic experience.

8. **Vegetables:** A variety of vegetables, such as eggplant, long beans, and Thai pumpkin, are commonly added to the curry, providing

texture and absorbing the flavours of the broth.

9. **Fish Sauce:** A fundamental element in Thai cuisine, fish sauce adds saltiness and umami, balancing the sour and spicy notes in the curry.

Cooking Process:

1. **Prepare the Broth Base:**

   - Begin by creating a flavorful broth base. Combine tamarind paste, shrimp paste, and water, allowing the ingredients to meld and form the foundation of the sour curry.

2. **Infuse Aromatics:**

   - Infuse the broth with aromatic elements. Lemongrass, galangal, and kaffir lime leaves are added to the pot, imparting their fragrant essence to the curry.

3. **Add Vegetables:**

   - Introduce a variety of vegetables to the simmering broth. The vegetables contribute both flavour and texture, absorbing the savoury and sour notes of the curry.

4. **Incorporate Fish:**

- Gently place the assorted fish into the broth, allowing it to cook and absorb the flavours. The choice of different fish varieties adds complexity to the curry.

5. **Adjust Spice Level:**

   - Adjust the spice level by incorporating Thai bird's eye chillies according to personal preferences. The chillies contribute a fiery kick that is characteristic of Southern Thai cuisine.

6. **Season with Fish Sauce:**

   - Season the curry with fish sauce, ensuring a harmonious balance of saltiness and umami. This step allows for customization based on individual taste preferences.

7. **Simmer to Perfection:**

   - Allow the curry to simmer, allowing the ingredients to meld and the flavours to intensify. The slow cooking process ensures that the fish becomes tender, and the vegetables absorb the essence of the curry.

Culinary Experience:

Gaeng Som Pla offers a culinary experience that is both invigorating and deeply satisfying. Each spoonful unveils a symphony of flavours—first, the sourness from tamarind, followed by the warmth of galangal, the herbal freshness of lemongrass, and the robust umami from the fish and shrimp paste. The medley of textures, from tender fish to crisp vegetables, adds a dynamic dimension to each bite.

Customization and Variations:

1. **Seafood Varieties:**

   - Experiment with different seafood varieties, such as prawns, squid, or crab, to create variations of Gaeng Som Pla. Each seafood choice contributes its unique flavours to the curry.

2. **Vegetarian Version:**

   - For a vegetarian version, omit the fish and shrimp paste, focusing on a selection of vibrant vegetables. The sour and aromatic elements of the curry can still shine without the inclusion of seafood.

3. **Pineapple Addition:**

   - Some variations of Gaeng Som Pla include pineapple chunks, adding a sweet and tangy element that complements the sourness of the tamarind.

Cultural Significance:

Gaeng Som Pla holds cultural significance in Southern Thailand, where it is not just a dish but a reflection of the region's bold and robust culinary identity. Often enjoyed as a centrepiece of family meals or festive gatherings, the curry embodies the spirit of communal dining and the joy of savouring intense and flavorful dishes together.

Presentation Tips:

1. **Bowl Arrangement:**

   - Serve Gaeng Som Pla in individual bowls, ensuring that each portion contains a generous serving of fish, vegetables, and aromatic broth.

2. **Vegetable Variety Showcase:**

   - Arrange the vegetables in a visually appealing manner, showcasing vibrant colours and textures. The diversity of vegetables adds to the visual allure of the curry.

3. **Garnish with Fresh Herbs:**

   - Garnish the curry with fresh cilantro or basil just before serving, adding a burst of greenery and an additional layer of aroma.

Global Appreciation:

The global appreciation for Thai cuisine extends to dishes like Gaeng Som Pla, which has found its way onto menus in Thai restaurants worldwide. Its distinctive combination of flavours has captivated international diners, offering a taste of Southern Thailand's culinary prowess.

Chapter 7: "Thai Sweets: A Sweet and Spicy Experience"

Exploration of traditional Thai desserts

Embarking on a sweet journey through Thailand unveils a delightful array of traditional desserts that reflect the country's rich culinary heritage and the artistry of Thai sweets. From the enchanting world of vibrant markets to the intricacies of family recipes passed down through generations, Thai desserts are a testament to the meticulous balance of flavours, textures, and cultural influences that define the nation's confectionery landscape.

1. Sticky Rice with Mango (Khao Niew Mamuang):

- This iconic Thai dessert is a harmonious blend of fragrant glutinous rice, coconut milk, and perfectly ripe mango slices. The sticky rice is soaked in coconut milk, imparting a creamy texture, and then paired with the luscious sweetness of mango. The dish is often garnished with sesame seeds or mung beans for added texture.

2. Coconut Sticky Rice with Custard (Khao Niew Sangkaya):

- A delectable variation of sticky rice, this dessert features a layer of smooth and velvety coconut custard atop a bed of glutinous rice. The custard is made with coconut milk, eggs, and palm sugar, creating a sweet and savoury combination. This indulgent treat is a favourite during festive occasions and family celebrations.

3. Thai Coconut Pudding (Khanom Thuai):

- Also known as "Thai jelly," Khanom Thuai is a delicate coconut pudding with a jelly-like consistency. The dessert is often moulded into small, flower-shaped cups and served with a drizzle of sweet palm syrup. The floral presentation adds an artistic touch to this light and refreshing sweet treat.

4. Thai Banana Fritters (Gluay Tod):

- A popular street food dessert, Gluay Tod features ripe bananas coated in a crispy, golden batter and deep-fried to perfection. The result is a delightful juxtaposition of a crunchy exterior and a tender, sweet banana inside. Often served with a dusting of sesame seeds or a side of coconut ice cream, these fritters are a beloved snack enjoyed across Thailand.

5. Thai Coconut Ice Cream (I-Tim Kati):

- I-Tim Kati offers a tropical twist on traditional ice cream, featuring coconut milk as a base. This creamy and fragrant treat is often served in a coconut shell or a cup, with a variety of toppings such as peanuts, sweet corn, or colourful sticky rice. The combination of rich coconut flavour and creative toppings makes it a refreshing and popular dessert.

6. Thai Pumpkin Custard (Sangkaya Fak Thong):

- This decadent dessert showcases the natural sweetness of pumpkin in a silky custard. The pumpkin is steamed and blended with coconut milk, eggs, and sugar, resulting in a velvety custard with a vibrant orange hue. Sangkaya Fak Thong is often topped with a drizzle of coconut cream and sesame seeds.

7. Black Sticky Rice with Coconut Cream (Khao Niew Dam):

- A classic Thai dessert, Khao Niew Dam features black glutinous rice cooked to a sticky consistency and drizzled with rich and creamy coconut cream. This dessert strikes a perfect balance between the nutty flavour of black rice and the indulgent sweetness of coconut cream.

8. Pandan Sticky Rice (Khao Niew Bai Toey):

- Pandan leaves lend their distinct fragrance and vibrant green colour to this variation of sticky rice. The pandan-infused rice is often paired with ripe mango or other tropical fruits, creating a visually appealing and aromatic dessert. It is a delightful representation of the use of natural ingredients in Thai sweets.

9. Taro Balls in Coconut Cream (Bua Loi):

- Bua Loi features chewy taro balls served in a warm and sweet coconut cream. The taro balls, made from a mixture of taro root and glutinous rice flour, offer a delightful texture, while the coconut cream provides a comforting and velvety finish. This dessert is both comforting and satisfying.

10. **Thai Sweet Roti (Roti Sai Mai):** - A playful and whimsical dessert, Roti Sai Mai consists of thin, crispy roti served with colourful strands of "sai mai," which are threads of sweet, flavoured sugar. The combination of crispy roti and delicate sugar threads

offers a delightful contrast in textures and a burst of sweetness.

Cultural Significance:

Thai desserts are deeply woven into the fabric of the country's culture and culinary traditions. Many of these sweets are associated with celebrations, religious ceremonies, and family gatherings. The intricate preparation and presentation of these desserts reflect the Thai people's attention to detail and their love for savouring life's sweet moments.

Artistic Presentation:

Thai desserts are not only a treat for the taste buds but also a feast for the eyes. The artful presentation often involves intricate moulding, shaping, and vibrant colours, showcasing the cultural importance placed on aesthetics. From flower-shaped coconut puddings to delicately crafted banana leaf wraps, the presentation of Thai desserts is an expression of culinary artistry.

Local Ingredients and Seasonality:

One of the defining characteristics of Thai desserts is the use of local and seasonal ingredients. Whether it's the abundance of tropical fruits, the fragrance of pandan leaves, or the richness of coconut milk, these desserts are a celebration of Thailand's diverse and bountiful natural resources.

Global Appreciation:

Thai desserts have garnered international acclaim, and many have become popular choices in Thai restaurants around the world. Their unique flavours, textures, and cultural significance have transcended borders, captivating the global sweet tooth and contributing to the widespread appreciation of Thai cuisine.

Discussion on the unique combination of sweetness and spiciness

The unique combination of sweetness and spiciness in Thai cuisine is a culinary masterpiece that tantalizes taste buds, creating a symphony of flavours that is as bold as it is harmonious. This distinctive balance, often referred to as the "Thai flavour profile," is a hallmark of the country's gastronomic identity, contributing to the allure and global popularity of Thai dishes. The interplay of sweetness and spiciness in Thai cuisine is not merely a matter of taste; it's a cultural phenomenon deeply rooted in the nation's history, geography, and the diverse array of ingredients that grace its kitchens.

The Sweetness Component:

1. **Palm Sugar and Sweetness:**

   - Palm sugar, derived from the sap of palm trees, is a fundamental sweetener in Thai cooking. Its rich and caramel-like flavour adds a natural sweetness to various dishes, from savoury curries to sweet desserts. The use of palm sugar imparts depth and complexity to Thai cuisine which sets it apart from other culinary traditions.

2. **Tropical Fruits as Sweeteners:**

   - Thailand's tropical climate gifts an abundance of sweet fruits, such as mangoes, pineapples, and lychees, which are often incorporated into both savoury and sweet dishes. The natural sweetness of these fruits not only enhances the overall flavour but also contributes to the vibrant and colourful presentation of Thai meals.

3. **Condiments and Sauces:**

   - Thai condiments and sauces often feature a sweet component. For example, hoisin sauce, oyster sauce, and sweet chilli sauce are prevalent in Thai cuisine, adding a layer of sweetness to stir-fries, dipping sauces, and glazes.

The Spiciness Component:

1. **Thai Chilies and Heat:**

   - Thai cuisine is renowned for its fiery heat, courtesy of Thai bird's eye chillies. These small but potent chillies are a key ingredient in many Thai dishes, providing the signature spiciness that Thai food is known for. The intensity of heat can vary,

allowing for a customizable spice
level to suit individual preferences.

2. **Curry Pastes and Spices:**

   - The foundation of many Thai curries
     lies in the intricately crafted curry
     pastes. These pastes, featuring a blend
     of spices like cumin, coriander, and
     peppercorns, contribute not only to
     the rich flavour but also to the
     lingering spiciness that characterizes
     Thai curries.

3. **Herbs like Basil and Mint:**

   - Aromatic herbs like Thai basil and
     mint bring a refreshing yet spicy kick
     to dishes. These herbs, often used as
     garnishes or in stir-fries, add a layer
     of complexity that complements the
     sweetness, creating a well-rounded
     flavour profile.

Harmonizing Sweetness and Spiciness:

1. **Balance in Thai Cuisine:**

   - The art of Thai cooking lies in
     achieving a delicate balance between
     sweetness and spiciness. It's not just
     about contrasting flavours but
     creating a synergy where each
     element enhances the other. This
     balance is evident in iconic dishes like
     Pad Thai, where tamarind provides a

sweet and sour note, while Thai chillies contribute the essential heat.

2. **Culinary Harmony:**

   - Thai chefs skillfully navigate the spectrum of flavours, ensuring that sweetness and spiciness coexist in perfect harmony. The result is a culinary experience where the palate is taken on a journey, from the initial burst of sweetness to the gradual crescendo of spiciness, creating a memorable and dynamic dining experience.

3. **Customization for Palate Preferences:**

   - One of the unique aspects of Thai cuisine is its adaptability to individual taste preferences. Many dishes are served with condiments like fish sauce, sugar, and crushed peanuts, allowing diners to adjust the sweetness and spiciness according to their liking. This customization adds a personal touch to the dining experience.

Cultural Significance:

1. **Reflection of Thai Culture:**

   - The balance of sweetness and spiciness in Thai cuisine reflects the multifaceted nature of Thai culture. It embodies the country's diverse landscapes, where tropical sweetness meets the fiery heat of spices. This culinary harmony mirrors the cultural richness and complexity that define Thailand.

2. **Celebration of Contrasts:**

   - Thai cuisine celebrates contrasts, both in flavours and textures. The marriage of sweet and spicy elements exemplifies the Thai philosophy of "yin and yang," where opposing forces come together to create a harmonious whole. This celebration of contrasts is deeply ingrained in the Thai way of life.

3. **Culinary Artistry:**

   - The artistry of Thai chefs lies in their ability to create a dance of flavours on the palate. The unique combination of sweetness and spiciness is not just a culinary technique; it's an expression of creativity and a testament to the craftsmanship embedded in Thai culinary traditions.

Global Appeal:

1. **International Influence:**

   - The global popularity of Thai cuisine can be attributed, in part, to the universal appeal of the sweet and spicy flavour profile. Thai restaurants worldwide have embraced this culinary trend, offering dishes that captivate diverse palates and contribute to the widespread love for Thai food.

2. **Culinary Fusion:**

   - The Thai penchant for balancing sweetness and spiciness has influenced culinary trends beyond the borders of Thailand. Chefs around the world incorporate Thai-inspired flavours into their dishes, creating a fusion of culinary traditions that resonate with a global audience.

3. **Consumer Preferences:**

   - The increasing demand for bold and adventurous flavours has elevated the appreciation for sweet and spicy combinations. Thai cuisine, with its masterful orchestration of these flavours, has become a go-to choice for those seeking a culinary experience that excites and satisfies them.

Recipe: "Sticky Rice with Mango" - Glutinous rice with mango

Delightfully simple yet profoundly satisfying, "Sticky Rice with Mango" or "Khao Niew Mamuang" epitomizes the harmonious marriage of textures and flavours in Thai desserts. This classic Thai delicacy brings together the lush sweetness of ripe mangoes with the creamy, glutinous richness of sticky rice, creating a dish that transcends its humble ingredients. Let's embark on a culinary journey to explore the art of crafting this beloved Thai dessert.

Ingredients:

1. **Glutinous Rice:** 2 cups of high-quality glutinous rice serve as the heart of this dish. The unique stickiness of this rice variety is essential for achieving the desired texture.

2. **Coconut Milk:** 1 can of coconut milk is a luscious component that infuses the sticky rice with a velvety richness. Choose a high-quality coconut milk for an authentic taste.

3. **Palm Sugar:** 1 cup of finely grated palm sugar contributes a natural sweetness with caramel undertones, imparting depth to the coconut milk drizzle.

4. **Salt:** A pinch of salt enhances the overall flavour profile, balancing the sweetness and adding a subtle savoury note to the dish.

5. **Sesame Seeds:** Toasted sesame seeds, sprinkled as a garnish, offer a nutty aroma

and an additional layer of texture to complement the creamy rice.

6. **Mangoes:** Select 3 to 4 ripe mangoes, preferably Thai varieties like Nam Dok Mai or Keo Savoy, known for their fragrant aroma and sweet, juicy flesh.

Cooking Process:

1. **Rinse and Soak the Rice:**

   - Begin by rinsing the glutinous rice under cold water until the water runs clear. Soak the rice in water for at least 4 hours or overnight to ensure it attains the desired sticky consistency.

2. **Steam the Rice:**

   - After soaking, drain the rice and place it in a bamboo or metal steamer lined with cheesecloth. Steam the rice over medium heat for approximately 25-30 minutes, or until it becomes tender and sticky.

3. **Prepare the Coconut Sauce:**

   - While the rice is steaming, heat the coconut milk in a saucepan over medium heat. Add the grated palm sugar and a pinch of salt, stirring continuously until the sugar dissolves, and the mixture forms a smooth, sweetened coconut sauce. Set aside to cool.

4. **Assemble the Dish:**

    - Once the rice is cooked, transfer it to a large bowl. While still hot, pour half of the coconut sauce over the rice, gently folding it in to ensure an even coating. Allow the rice to absorb the coconut sauce, enhancing its flavour and stickiness.

5. **Peel and Slice Mangoes:**

    - Peel the ripe mangoes and slice them into thin, elegant strips. The vibrant colour and juiciness of the mangoes will complement the richness of the sticky rice.

6. **Serve and Garnish:**

    - To serve, mould a portion of the sticky rice on a plate or in a small bowl. Arrange the mango slices alongside or on top of the rice. Drizzle the remaining coconut sauce over the dish, allowing it to cascade down the sides. Sprinkle toasted sesame seeds for a final touch.

Culinary Experience:

The first spoonful of Sticky Rice with Mango is a sensorial delight. The glutinous rice, infused with the sweet coconut sauce, exhibits a satisfying chewiness, while the ripe mango slices provide bursts of juicy sweetness. The amalgamation of creamy coconut, sticky rice, and succulent mango creates a palate-pleasing experience that encapsulates the essence of Thai dessert craftsmanship.

Customization and Variations:

1. **Add Pandan Flavor:**

    - For an additional layer of aroma, infuse the coconut sauce with pandan leaves during heating. The subtle, fragrant notes of pandan elevate the dish's overall sensory appeal.

2. **Top with Mung Beans:**

    - In traditional Thai fashion, sprinkle cooked and sweetened mung beans over the sticky rice for a delightful crunch and added sweetness.

3. **Coconut Ice Cream Companion:**

    - For an indulgent twist, serve the Sticky Rice with Mango alongside a scoop of coconut ice cream. The contrast in temperatures and textures creates a heavenly dessert experience.

Cultural Significance:

Sticky Rice with Mango is not just a dessert; it is a cultural icon embedded in Thai culinary traditions. Often enjoyed during the mango season, which aligns with the Thai New Year, the dish symbolizes prosperity, abundance, and the sweetness of life's fleeting moments.

Presentation Tips:

1. **Artful Plating:**

   - Artfully arrange the mango slices on the plate, creating a visual feast for the eyes. The vibrant colours of the mango against the creamy rice evoke a tropical paradise.

2. **Drizzle Elegance:**

   - Drizzle the coconut sauce with precision, allowing it to cascade gracefully over the rice. The careful presentation adds an element of elegance to the dish.

3. **Garnish with Precision:**

   - Sprinkle toasted sesame seeds with precision, ensuring an even distribution for both visual appeal and a nuanced nutty flavour.

Global Appreciation:

The global appeal of Sticky Rice with Mango lies in its simple, yet complex flavour profile. Found on Thai restaurant menus worldwide, it has become a beloved representation of Thai culinary finesse and the perfect embodiment of the sweet and sticky delights that Thai desserts offer.

Chapter 8: "The Perfect Dinner: Complete Thai Menu"

Guide to creating a complete menu with different dishes

Creating a complete Thai menu is an art form that goes beyond the mere arrangement of dishes; it's a culinary journey that invites diners to savour the diverse and vibrant flavours of Thailand. A well-curated Thai menu embodies the essence of Thai cuisine—bold, aromatic, and intricately balanced. From appetizers that awaken the palate to savoury main courses and delightful desserts, each dish contributes to a symphony of tastes that reflects the richness of Thai culinary traditions.

1. **Appetizers:**

- **a. Thai Spring Rolls (Por Pia Tod):**

  - These crispy spring rolls are filled with a delectable mixture of vegetables, glass noodles, and sometimes minced meat. Served with a sweet and tangy dipping sauce, they set the stage for the culinary journey to come.

- **b. Som Tum (Green Papaya Salad):**

  - A refreshing and spicy salad featuring shredded green papaya, cherry tomatoes, green beans, and peanuts, all tossed in a zesty dressing. Som

Tum adds a burst of vibrant flavours, balancing sweetness, sourness, and heat.

- **c. Satay Skewers with Peanut Sauce:**

  - Grilled skewers of marinated meat, often chicken or beef, served with a luscious peanut sauce. The smoky aroma of the grill and the rich nuttiness of the sauce create a tantalizing appetizer.

2. **Main Courses:**

- **a. Pad Thai:**

  - A quintessential Thai noodle dish that combines stir-fried rice noodles with a medley of ingredients like tofu, shrimp, or chicken. The flavours are harmonized with tamarind paste, fish sauce, and lime, offering a perfect balance of sweet, sour, and savoury.

- **b. Green Curry Chicken (Gaeng Keow Wan Gai):**

  - A fragrant and mildly spicy green curry featuring tender chicken, Thai eggplants, and aromatic herbs like basil and kaffir lime leaves. The coconut milk-based curry provides a creamy backdrop to vibrant flavours.

- **c. Pad Krapow Moo (Stir-fried Pork with Basil):**

- A flavorful stir-fry of minced pork, garlic, chillies, and holy basil. This dish showcases the bold and aromatic nature of Thai cuisine, with a perfect blend of spiciness and herbal notes.

- **d. Pla Rad Prik (Fried Fish with Spicy Sauce):**

  - Crispy-fried fish served with a spicy chilli sauce that adds a punch to the delicate flavours of the fish. The contrast of textures and the boldness of the sauce make it a standout seafood dish.

- **e. Khao Soi (Curry Noodle Soup from the North):**

  - Hailing from Northern Thailand, Khao Soi is a rich and aromatic curry noodle soup. The combination of coconut milk, curry spices, and crispy noodles creates a multi-layered culinary experience.

3. **Side Dishes:**

- **a. Som Tum Tod (Crispy Green Papaya Salad):**

  - A variation of Som Tum where the green papaya is thinly sliced and deep-fried, offering a delightful contrast of crispy texture to the

113

familiar flavours of green papaya salad.

- **b. Pad Pak Boong (Stir-fried Morning Glory):**

  - Stir-fried morning glory, a leafy green vegetable, with garlic, chilli, and oyster sauce. This side dish adds freshness and crunch to the meal.

- **c. Khao Niew (Sticky Rice):**

  - Essential in Thai cuisine, sticky rice is served as a side to soak up the flavours of main dishes. Its unique texture complements the sauciness of curries and stir-fries.

4. **Desserts:**

- **a. Mango with Sticky Rice (Khao Niew Mamuang):**

  - A classic Thai dessert featuring ripe mango slices served atop sticky rice drizzled with sweet coconut milk. The contrast of warm rice and cool, juicy mango creates a blissful finale to the meal.

- **b. Tub Tim Grob (Water Chestnuts in Coconut Milk):**

  - A refreshing and sweet dessert with water chestnut cubes coated in vibrant colours, served in sweetened coconut milk with ice. It provides a cool and textural contrast to the warm, savoury dishes.

- **c. Khanom Krok (Coconut Pancakes):**
  - Small, bite-sized coconut pancakes with a slightly crispy exterior and a soft, gooey centre. These delightful treats offer a sweet conclusion to the meal.

5. Beverages:

- **a. Thai Iced Tea (Cha Yen):**
  - A sweet and creamy iced tea made with strongly brewed Thai tea, sweetened condensed milk, and evaporated milk. The distinctive orange hue and the combination of sweet and bitter notes make it a popular Thai beverage.

- **b. Lemongrass and Pandan Cooler:**
  - A refreshing non-alcoholic beverage made by infusing lemongrass and pandan leaves in water, sweetening with simple syrup, and serving over ice. It provides a crisp and aromatic respite.

- **c. Thai Basil Seed Drink (Nam Manglak):**
  - A unique and nutritious drink made by soaking basil seeds in water until

they form a gelatinous texture. Sweetened with sugar or honey, it offers a refreshing and mildly sweet taste.

Culinary Harmony and Presentation: Creating a complete Thai menu is not just about the individual dishes but also about achieving a harmonious balance in flavours, textures, and colours. The menu should take diners on a sensory journey, progressing seamlessly from appetizers that awaken the palate to rich and satisfying main courses, and concluding with delightful desserts that leave a lasting impression.

Cultural Significance: A well-crafted Thai menu reflects the cultural diversity of the country, incorporating regional specialities and traditional ingredients. It pays homage to the culinary traditions passed down through generations, celebrating the unique flavours that define Thai cuisine.

Presentation Tips:

1. **Visual Appeal:**

   - Pay attention to the visual presentation of each dish. Vibrant colours, garnishes, and thoughtful plating enhance the dining experience and create an inviting visual feast.

2. **Family-Style Dining:**

   - Consider a family-style dining approach, where dishes are placed in the centre for sharing. This fosters a

communal atmosphere, allowing
diners to sample a variety of flavours.

3. **Balance in Flavors and Textures:**

    - Ensure a balance of flavours and
      textures throughout the menu. The
      interplay of sweet and savoury,
      crunchy and tender, creates a
      dynamic dining experience.

Global Appreciation: Thai cuisine has achieved
global acclaim for its bold and exciting flavours. A
well-crafted Thai menu is not only appreciated by
those familiar with Thai culture but also introduces
new enthusiasts to the diverse and delicious world of
Thai culinary artistry.

Tips on pairing dishes for an authentic culinary experience

Creating an authentic Thai culinary experience goes
beyond individual recipes; it's about orchestrating a
symphony of flavours that dance harmoniously on the
palate. Thai cuisine, renowned for its bold and diverse
taste profile, offers a plethora of ingredients and
techniques that, when thoughtfully combined, elevate
the dining experience to new heights. Here are tips on
pairing dishes to create an immersive and authentic
Thai culinary journey.

1. **Consider Regional Specialties:**

    - Thai cuisine is diverse, with distinct regional
      specialities reflecting the unique

characteristics of each area. Consider grouping dishes that share regional roots to provide a more immersive experience. For example, pair Northern Thai Khao Soi with Chiang Mai sausage for an authentic taste of the region.

2. Balance Heat Levels:

- Thai cuisine is known for its spiciness, but achieving a balance is key. Pair milder dishes, such as Pad Thai or Green Curry, with more fiery options like Som Tum (Green Papaya Salad) or Pad Krapow Moo (Stir-fried Pork with Basil). This ensures a gradual progression of heat throughout the meal.

3. Contrast Textures:

- Thai cuisine excels in contrasting textures, creating a delightful sensory experience. Pair crispy dishes like Thai Spring Rolls or Pad Thai with softer, saucier options such as Green Curry or Tom Kha Gai (Chicken Coconut Soup). The interplay of crunchy and tender enhances the overall dining adventure.

4. Harmonize Sweet and Savory:

- Thai dishes often strike a perfect balance between sweet and savoury. Pair sweet and tangy Som Tum (Green Papaya Salad) with savoury and rich Gaeng Keow Wan Gai (Green Curry Chicken) to create a complementary flavour profile that is quintessentially Thai.

5. Mindful Rice Pairing:

- Rice is a staple in Thai cuisine, and the type of rice can impact the dining experience. Pair fragrant Jasmine rice with dishes that have bold, flavorful sauces, such as Massaman Curry or Panang Curry. Sticky rice, on the other hand, complements grilled or saucy dishes like Moo Ping (Grilled Pork Skewers) or Pla Rad Prik (Fried Fish with Spicy Sauce).

6. Explore Seafood Varieties:

- Thailand's coastal regions offer an abundance of fresh seafood. Pair seafood-centric dishes like Tom Yum Goong (Spicy Shrimp Soup) or Pla Tod Rad Prik (Fried Fish with Chili Sauce) with lighter options such as Yum Talay (Seafood Salad) to showcase the variety and freshness of Thai seafood.

7. Accentuate Aromatics:

- Thai cuisine relies heavily on aromatic herbs and spices. Pair dishes that feature similar herbs, such as basil or cilantro, to create a cohesive aromatic experience. For example, pair Pad Krapow Moo (Stir-fried Pork with Basil) with Tom Yum (Spicy and Sour Soup) for an herbal symphony.

8. Family-Style Dining:

- Embrace the Thai tradition of family-style dining, where multiple dishes are placed in the centre for sharing. This communal approach allows diners to experience a variety of flavours in one sitting, fostering a sense of togetherness and exploration.

9. Consider Textile Palate Cleansers:

- Introduce dishes that act as palate cleansers between bolder flavours. For instance, Som Tum Tod (Crispy Green Papaya Salad) can refresh the palate after indulging in richer dishes like Gaeng Massaman Nua (Massaman Beef Curry).

10. **Mindful Beverage Pairing:** - Pair Thai dishes with traditional beverages to enhance the overall dining experience. Thai Iced Tea (Cha Yen) complements spicy dishes, while Lemongrass and Pandan Cooler provide a refreshing contrast to richer curries.

11. **Seasonal Sensibilities:** - Consider the seasonality of ingredients when pairing dishes. Highlight fresh, seasonal produce in salads like Yum Woon Sen (Glass Noodle Salad) during warmer months, and opt for heartier stews like Gaeng Hang Lay (Northern Thai Pork Curry) in cooler seasons.

12. **Explore Vegetarian and Meat Options:** - Accommodate diverse preferences by offering a balance of vegetarian and meat-based dishes. Pair vegetable-centric choices like Pad Pak Boong (Stir-fried Morning Glory) with meatier options such as Gai Tod (Thai Fried Chicken) for a well-rounded menu.

Cultural Context: Thai cuisine is deeply rooted in cultural traditions, and understanding the context can enhance the pairing experience. Consider the occasion—whether it's a festive celebration or a casual gathering—and tailor the menu accordingly. Embrace the Thai philosophy of balance, where each dish contributes to a harmonious whole.

Presentation Matters: Pay attention to the visual presentation of the dishes. Vibrant colours, thoughtful garnishes, and an artful arrangement contribute to the overall dining experience. Create a feast for the eyes that complements the symphony of flavours.

Adapt to Dietary Preferences: Accommodate dietary preferences and restrictions by offering a diverse selection of dishes. Clearly label vegetarian, vegan, and gluten-free options to ensure all diners can partake in the culinary journey.

Educate and Engage: Consider providing brief descriptions or anecdotes about each dish on the menu. This not only educates diners about the flavours they can expect but also adds a storytelling element, enhancing their connection to the culinary experience.

Reflections on the growth of culinary skills through the preparation of Thai dishes

Embarking on the journey of preparing Thai dishes is not just a culinary exploration; it is a transformative odyssey that unravels layers of flavours, techniques, and cultural nuances. The growth experienced through mastering the art of Thai cuisine extends beyond the kitchen, leaving an indelible mark on one's culinary skills, appreciation for diverse ingredients, and a deeper understanding of the cultural tapestry that weaves through each dish.

1. **Mastery of Flavor Harmony:**

- Thai cuisine is renowned for its intricate balance of sweet, savoury, spicy, and sour flavours—a harmony that distinguishes it on the global culinary stage. The journey of preparing Thai dishes becomes a lesson in achieving this delicate equilibrium. From crafting the perfect Pad Thai with its nuanced tamarind and lime dance to infusing a Green Curry Chicken with aromatic herbs, every dish is a brushstroke on the canvas of flavour mastery.

2. **Technique Precision and Versatility:**

- Thai cooking introduces a rich tapestry of techniques that elevate one's culinary skills. From the precision of knife skills in creating uniform vegetable slices for dishes like Som Tum to the art of stir-frying that imparts a smoky depth to Pad Krapow Moo, each technique is a gateway to a broader culinary skill set. The versatility required to navigate the diversity of Thai dishes—from delicate salads to robust curries—forges a well-rounded culinary prowess.

3. **Ingredient Appreciation and Exploration:**

- Thai cuisine celebrates an extensive array of ingredients, many of which may be new and exotic to those outside of Thailand. The journey of preparing Thai dishes becomes a treasure hunt through local markets and speciality stores, exploring galangal, kaffir lime leaves, and Thai bird's eye chillies. This exploration instils a profound appreciation for the role each ingredient plays in creating the symphony of Thai flavours.

4. Cultural Connection through Cuisine:

- Thai cooking is not just about recipes; it is a cultural expression deeply rooted in traditions and local wisdom. The preparation of Thai dishes becomes a bridge to understanding the cultural significance of ingredients, rituals, and culinary practices. It's a journey that transcends taste, offering a glimpse into the rich heritage and everyday life of the Thai people.

5. Sensory Sensitivity and Adaptability:

- The sensory journey of preparing Thai dishes hones one's ability to be attuned to flavours, aromas, and textures. From balancing the heat in a Tom Yum Goong to discerning the subtleties of different curry pastes, this heightened sensory sensitivity becomes a valuable skill that transcends Thai cuisine, enriching one's overall culinary repertoire.

6. Culinary Confidence and Creativity:

- As the mastery of Thai dishes progresses, a newfound culinary confidence emerges. The ability to navigate complex recipes, adapt flavours to personal preferences, and even experiment with innovative twists on traditional dishes blossoms. This sense of confidence extends beyond Thai cuisine, empowering individuals to approach the kitchen with creativity and a willingness to explore diverse culinary traditions.

7. Cross-Cultural Culinary Fluency:

- The preparation of Thai dishes opens a gateway to cross-cultural culinary fluency. The skills acquired in understanding Thai flavours, techniques, and cultural nuances provide a foundation for exploring other global cuisines with greater ease and appreciation. It becomes a testament to the interconnected nature of culinary traditions worldwide.

8. Adventurous Palate Development:

- Thai cuisine, with its bold and adventurous flavour combinations, serves as a playground for palate development. The journey of preparing Thai dishes transforms the palate, cultivating an appreciation for bold spices, aromatic herbs, and the delicate dance between sweet, savoury, and spicy. This newfound adventurous palate extends to an openness to explore and appreciate a wide spectrum of flavours from around the world.

9. Community and Culinary Sharing:

- The preparation of Thai dishes transcends the solitary act of cooking; it becomes a communal experience. Whether cooking for friends, family, or a wider community, sharing Thai dishes becomes a gesture of cultural exchange and connection. It's a journey that extends beyond personal growth, fostering a sense of community through the universal language of food.

10. **Mindful Eating and Gratitude:** - Thai cuisine places a strong emphasis on mindfulness in both preparation and consumption. The journey of preparing Thai dishes instils a sense of mindfulness, encouraging awareness of each ingredient's contribution and the appreciation of the effort put into crafting a dish. This mindfulness extends to dining experiences, fostering a deeper sense of gratitude for the culinary journey undertaken.

11. **Culinary Resilience and Adaptation:** - The preparation of Thai dishes often involves navigating unfamiliar techniques and ingredients. This journey becomes a lesson in culinary resilience and adaptation—skills that prove invaluable in the ever-evolving world of cooking. Overcoming challenges and embracing the unknown become integral aspects of the culinary growth experience.

12. **Lifetime Learning and Exploration:** - The journey of preparing Thai dishes is not a destination but a continuous exploration. The dynamic nature of Thai cuisine, influenced by regional variations and seasonal ingredients, encourages a lifetime of

learning. It becomes a journey where each dish crafted is a stepping stone to discovering new facets of Thai culinary artistry.

Conclusion

Summary of key points on elevating culinary skills through Thai cooking

Engaging in the world of Thai cooking is not just about creating flavorful dishes; it is a transformative journey that elevates culinary skills to new heights. From mastering the delicate art of flavour balance to embracing diverse techniques and ingredients, Thai cooking offers a rich tapestry for culinary exploration. Let's delve into key points that encapsulate the essence of elevating culinary skills through the vibrant and dynamic realm of Thai cuisine.

1. **Mastery of Flavor Harmony:**

- Thai cooking is a masterclass in achieving flavour harmony. The key lies in balancing sweet, savoury, spicy, and sour notes within each dish. Learning to navigate this intricate dance of flavours not only enhances Thai culinary skills but also provides a foundation for creating well-balanced dishes across various cuisines.

2. **Technique Precision and Versatility:**

- Thai cuisine introduces a diverse range of culinary techniques, from the precision of knife skills to the art of stir-frying and the delicate balance of steaming. Mastery of these techniques not only imparts a versatile skill set but also enhances precision and finesse in the kitchen.

3. **Ingredient Appreciation and Exploration:**

- Thai cooking is a celebration of diverse and exotic ingredients. The journey involves exploring markets for galangal, kaffir lime leaves, and Thai chillies, fostering a deep appreciation for the role each ingredient plays in crafting authentic Thai flavours. This exploration broadens culinary horizons and encourages a lifelong curiosity about global ingredients.

4. **Cultural Connection through Cuisine:**

- Thai cooking goes beyond recipes; it is a cultural exploration deeply rooted in traditions. Understanding the cultural context behind each dish fosters a connection to the rich heritage of Thailand. This cultural immersion adds depth to culinary skills, providing a holistic understanding of the dishes being prepared.

5. Sensory Sensitivity and Adaptability:

- The sensory journey in Thai cooking refines sensitivity to flavours, aromas, and textures. The ability to discern the subtleties in Thai cuisine hones sensory skills and fosters adaptability in the kitchen. This heightened sensitivity becomes a valuable asset in crafting nuanced dishes and exploring diverse culinary traditions.

6. Culinary Confidence and Creativity:

- As proficiency in Thai cooking grows, so does culinary confidence. The ability to navigate complex recipes and experiment with flavours fosters creativity in the kitchen. Thai cooking becomes a canvas for culinary expression, empowering individuals to infuse their unique twists into traditional dishes.

7. Cross-Cultural Culinary Fluency:

- Thai cooking acts as a gateway to cross-cultural culinary fluency. The skills acquired in mastering Thai flavours and techniques lay a foundation for exploring other global cuisines with ease. This cross-cultural culinary understanding reflects the interconnected nature of culinary traditions worldwide.

8. Adventurous Palate Development:

- Thai cuisine, with its bold and adventurous flavour combinations, transforms the palate. The journey of tasting and preparing Thai dishes cultivate an adventurous palate, fostering an appreciation for bold spices, aromatic herbs, and diverse textures. This newfound palate extends to a willingness to explore a wide spectrum of global flavours.

9. **Community and Culinary Sharing:** - Thai cooking transcends individual efforts; it is a communal experience that fosters connection and cultural exchange. Sharing Thai dishes becomes an act of culinary generosity, creating a sense of community through the universal language of food.

10. **Mindful Eating and Gratitude:** - Thai cooking instils mindfulness, both in preparation and consumption. The journey involves appreciating each ingredient's contribution and expressing gratitude for the culinary process. This mindfulness extends to dining experiences, fostering a deeper connection to the food being enjoyed.

11. **Culinary Resilience and Adaptation:** - Thai cooking often involves navigating unfamiliar techniques and ingredients, cultivating culinary resilience. Overcoming challenges and adapting to

new culinary landscapes become integral components of the learning journey. These skills contribute to a chef's ability to thrive in the ever-evolving world of cooking.

12. **Lifetime Learning and Exploration:** - The journey of Thai cooking is an ongoing exploration. The dynamic nature of Thai cuisine, influenced by regional variations and seasonal ingredients, encourages a lifetime of learning. Each dish prepared becomes a stepping stone to discovering new facets of Thai culinary artistry.

Invitation to further experiment with recipes and explore other culinary traditions

As you savour the vibrant and tantalizing flavours of Thai cuisine, consider this an invitation to extend your culinary journey beyond the boundaries of recipes and explore the rich tapestry of global gastronomy. Thai cooking has undoubtedly bestowed upon you a wealth of skills and a palate attuned to bold and diverse flavours. Now, let's take this newfound culinary expertise as a passport to embark on an exciting adventure of experimentation and exploration.

1. **Thai Recipe Remix:**

- Armed with the skills acquired from Thai cooking, why not embark on a journey of recipe remixing? Take the foundational principles of Thai flavours—the delicate balance of sweet, savoury, spicy, and sour—

and apply them to dishes from other culinary traditions. Imagine a tangy Thai-infused pasta or a savoury Thai-inspired pizza. Let your creativity run wild as you fuse Thai elements with your favourite global recipes.

2. Global Fusion:

- Thai cuisine's ability to harmonize diverse flavours makes it an ideal companion for culinary fusion. Explore the art of blending Thai ingredients with those from other cuisines. Picture a Thai-spiced taco with a zesty mango salsa or a fragrant Thai-infused risotto. By merging Thai flavours with dishes from around the world, you create a culinary symphony that transcends borders.

3. Flavor-Infused Grilling:

- Thai grilling techniques, as showcased in dishes like Moo Ping (Grilled Pork Skewers), provide a wonderful foundation for experimenting with other grilled delights. Apply Thai marinades and spice blends to meats and vegetables destined for the grill. Whether it's Thai-inspired kebabs or grilled seafood with a lemongrass twist, let the grill become your canvas for global flavour exploration.

4. Dive into Asian Cuisine:

- Thai cuisine is just one facet of the rich and diverse tapestry of Asian culinary traditions. Take a culinary journey through neighbouring countries like Vietnam, Malaysia, or Indonesia. Explore the aromatic spices of Indonesian Rendang, the refreshing flavours of Vietnamese Pho, or the complex layers of Malaysian Laksa. Each dish unveils a new chapter in the story of Asian gastronomy.

5. Mediterranean Magic:

- Imagine infusing the bold Thai flavours you've mastered into the sun-kissed dishes of the Mediterranean. Experiment with Thai-inspired tapenades, vibrant herb-infused salads, or grilled meats with a Thai twist. By marrying the freshness of Mediterranean ingredients with the zest of Thai spices, you create a fusion that tantalizes the taste buds.

6. Latin American Fusion:

- Latin American cuisine is a celebration of bold flavours and vibrant colours. Merge Thai spices with the warmth of Latin American dishes. Picture Thai-infused ceviche, coconut milk-based Thai arepas or a spicy Thai-inspired salsa. Unleash the potential of combining these two culinary worlds for a fiesta of flavours.

7. Middle Eastern Medley:

- Transport your taste buds to the aromatic landscapes of the Middle East by infusing Thai elements into traditional dishes. Imagine a Thai-inspired hummus, a zesty tabbouleh with a lemongrass kick, or a Thai-spiced grilled lamb. The convergence of Middle Eastern and Thai flavours creates a symphony of tastes that resonate across continents.

8. African Adventure:

- Explore the diverse cuisines of Africa and weave Thai influences into the rich tapestry of flavours. Picture a Thai-spiced peri-peri chicken, a fragrant North African tagine with Thai herbs, or a Thai-infused bobotie from South Africa. By embracing the culinary diversity of the African continent, you embark on a flavorful journey that spans borders.

9. **European Elegance:** - Thai cuisine, with its precision and attention to detail, complements the refined elegance of European dishes. Experiment with Thai-inspired sauces for pasta, infuse Thai herbs into French classics or add a spicy Thai twist to Spanish paella. The fusion of Thai and European culinary traditions creates a culinary dialogue that transcends cultural boundaries.

10. **Sweet Concoctions:** - Thai desserts, with their unique combination of sweetness and aromatic richness, provide inspiration for sweet experiments. Explore Thai-infused pastries, cakes, and ice creams. Picture a basil-infused crème brûlée or a lemongrass-scented tart. The fusion of Thai dessert elements with Western sweets opens up a world of delightful possibilities.

11. **Plant-Based Exploration:** - Thai cuisine offers a rich canvas for plant-based experimentation. Explore the world of Thai-inspired vegetarian and vegan dishes. Transform classics like Pad Thai or Green Curry into plant-powered delights. By embracing plant-based ingredients, you not only expand your culinary repertoire but also contribute to a sustainable and vibrant culinary landscape.

12. **Interactive Culinary Gatherings:** - Turn your kitchen into a global culinary hub by hosting interactive gatherings. Invite friends and family to join in the experimentation. Create a themed menu that fuses Thai elements with dishes from different culinary traditions. This shared culinary experience becomes a celebration of diversity, flavour, and the joy of exploring new gastronomic horizons together.

Closing with encouragement to enjoy the results of the culinary journey through Thailand

As you wrap up your delightful sojourn into the realms of Thai cuisine, let this moment be more than just the end of a culinary adventure—it's a celebration of your newfound skills, a testament to your creative spirit, and an invitation to savour the delectable results of your Thai culinary journey. Take a moment to relish the unique flavours, aromatic wonders, and cultural richness that you've woven into each dish. Here's a heartfelt encouragement to fully enjoy the fruits of your labour and celebrate the culinary triumph you've achieved.

1. Culinary Self-Appreciation:

- Before you indulge in the feast before you, take a moment to appreciate your culinary journey. Recognize the growth in your skills, the creativity you've unleashed in the kitchen, and the cultural connections you've fostered through Thai cooking. Your dedication has transformed mere ingredients into a symphony of flavours that dance on the palate.

2. Embrace the Thai Dining Experience:

- Thai dining is not just about the food; it's a holistic experience that engages all the senses. Set the mood with vibrant table settings, immerse yourself in the fragrant aromas wafting from the dishes, and relish the visual feast of colours that Thai cuisine brings to the table. Create an atmosphere that mirrors the lively spirit of Thai culinary traditions.

3. Celebrate with Loved Ones:

- Food is a universal language of celebration and connection. Share your culinary triumph with loved ones. Invite friends or family to join in the feast and let the joy of Thai flavours become a shared experience. The act of sharing transcends the dining table, fostering a sense of togetherness and creating lasting memories.

4. Capture the Culinary Moments:

- Take a moment to capture the essence of your culinary creations. Snap photos of the beautifully plated dishes, the vibrant colours, and the smiles of satisfaction around the table. Documenting your culinary journey creates a visual narrative that you can revisit, cherishing the memories of the time and effort invested in mastering Thai recipes.

5. Reflect on Your Culinary Growth:

- As you savour each bite, reflect on the culinary growth you've experienced. Consider the techniques you've mastered, the ingredients you've come to appreciate, and the cultural insights you've gained through the preparation of authentic Thai dishes. Your journey extends beyond the kitchen; it's a reflection of your evolving culinary prowess.

6. Bask in the Joy of Creativity:

- The kitchen is your canvas, and Thai cuisine has provided the palette for your culinary creativity. Bask in the joy of unleashing your imagination, whether it's through innovative twists on traditional recipes, flavour fusions with global influences, or the artful presentation of each dish. Your culinary creations are a testament to the artist within you.

7. Gratitude for Cultural Exploration:

- Express gratitude for the cultural exploration woven into each recipe. Thai cuisine is a gateway to understanding the traditions, flavours, and everyday life of the Thai people. Your commitment to authenticity and cultural respect has not only resulted in delicious dishes but also deepened your connection to the global culinary mosaic.

8. Share Culinary Stories:

- Every dish has a story, and your Thai culinary journey is no exception. Share the stories behind your favourite recipes, the challenges you overcame, and the moments of culinary triumph. Engage in the joy of storytelling around the dining table, creating a narrative that extends beyond the flavours on the plate.

9. **Appreciate the Fusion of Flavors:** - Celebrate the fusion of Thai flavours with your own culinary preferences. Whether you've added a personal twist to a classic recipe or infused global influences into Thai dishes, appreciate the harmonious blend of diverse tastes. Your kitchen has become a melting pot of flavours, and each dish tells a unique story.

10. **Extend the Culinary Journey:** - The closing of one culinary chapter marks the beginning of countless possibilities. As you enjoy the fruits of your Thai culinary journey, consider how you can extend this exploration. Perhaps there are new Thai recipes to conquer, or you may be inspired to delve into the

culinary traditions of another region. Let your kitchen be a perpetual playground for culinary discovery.

11. **Toast to Culinary Adventures:** - Raise a glass in a symbolic toast to your culinary adventures. Whether it's a refreshing Thai-inspired beverage or a favourite drink of your choice, celebrate the joy of creating, experimenting, and indulging in the rich tapestry of Thai flavours. This moment is a culmination of dedication, creativity, and the sheer pleasure of cooking.

12. **Future Culinary Triumphs:** - As you conclude this chapter of Thai culinary exploration, anticipate the many culinary triumphs that lie ahead. Your journey is a continuous odyssey of growth, learning, and savouring the myriad flavours that the world of food has to offer. The kitchen is your playground, and each dish is an opportunity for future culinary triumphs.